HBR'S 10 MUST READS

On
Leadership
(Vol. 2)

HBR's 10 Must Reads series is the definitive collection of ideas and best practices for aspiring and experienced leaders alike. These books offer essential reading selected from the pages of *Harvard Business Review* on topics critical to the success of every manager.

Titles include:

HBR's 10 Must Reads 2015
HBR's 10 Must Reads 2016
HBR's 10 Must Reads 2017
HBR's 10 Must Reads 2018
HBR's 10 Must Reads 2019
HBR's 10 Must Reads 2020
HBR's 10 Must Reads for CEOs
HBR's 10 Must Reads for New Managers
HBR's 10 Must Reads on AI, Analytics, and the New Machine Age
HBR's 10 Must Reads on Boards
HBR's 10 Must Reads on Business Model Innovation
HBR's 10 Must Reads on Change Management
HBR's 10 Must Reads on Collaboration
HBR's 10 Must Reads on Communication
HBR's 10 Must Reads on Design Thinking
HBR's 10 Must Reads on Diversity
HBR's 10 Must Reads on Emotional Intelligence
HBR's 10 Must Reads on Entrepreneurship and Startups
HBR's 10 Must Reads on Innovation
HBR's 10 Must Reads on Leadership
HBR's 10 Must Reads on Leadership (Vol. 2)
HBR's 10 Must Reads on Leadership for Healthcare
HBR's 10 Must Reads on Leadership Lessons from Sports
HBR's 10 Must Reads on Making Smart Decisions
HBR's 10 Must Reads on Managing Across Cultures
HBR's 10 Must Reads on Managing in a Downturn
HBR's 10 Must Reads on Managing People
HBR's 10 Must Reads on Managing People (Vol. 2)
HBR's 10 Must Reads on Managing Risk

On Leadership
(Vol. 2)

HARVARD BUSINESS REVIEW PRESS
Boston, Massachusetts

Library of Congress Cataloging-in-Publication data

Title: HBR's 10 must reads on leadership. Vol. 2.
Other titles: On leadership. Vol. 2. | HBR's 10 must reads (Series)
Description: Boston, Massachusetts : Harvard Business Review Press, [2020] | Series: HBR's 10 must reads | Includes index. |
Identifiers: LCCN 2019042298 (print) | LCCN 2019042299 (ebook) | ISBN 9781633699106 (paperback) | ISBN 9781633699113 (ebook)
Subjects: LCSH: Leadership.
Classification: LCC HD57.7 .H3916 2020 (print) | LCC HD57.7 (ebook) | DDC 658.4/092—dc23
LC record available at https://lccn.loc.gov/2019042298
LC ebook record available at https://lccn.loc.gov/2019042299

ISBN: 978-1-63369-910-6
eISBN: 978-1-63369-911-3

Contents

**HBR'S
10
MUST
READS**

On
Leadership
(Vol. 2)

Leadership Is a Conversation

by Boris Groysberg and Michael Slind

THE COMMAND-AND-CONTROL APPROACH to management has in recent years become less and less viable. Globalization, new technologies, and changes in how companies create value and interact with customers have sharply reduced the efficacy of a purely directive, top-down model of leadership. What will take the place of that model? Part of the answer lies in how leaders manage communication within their organizations—that is, how they handle the flow of information to, from, and among their employees. Traditional corporate communication must give way to a process that is more dynamic and more sophisticated. Most important, that process must be *conversational*.

We arrived at that conclusion while conducting a recent research project that focused on the state of organizational communication in the 21st century. Over more than two years we interviewed professional communicators as well as top leaders at a variety of organizations—large and small, blue chip and start-up, for-profit and nonprofit, U.S. and international. To date we have spoken with nearly 150 people at more than 100 companies. Both implicitly and explicitly, participants in our research mentioned their efforts to "have a conversation" with their people or their ambition to "advance the conversation" within their companies. Building upon the insights and examples gleaned from this research, we have developed a model of leadership that we call "organizational conversation."

Elements of organizational conversation

Intimacy	Interactivity	Inclusion	Intentionality
How leaders relate to employees	*How leaders use communication channels*	*How leaders develop organizational content*	*How leaders convey strategy*
Old model: corporate communication			
Information flow is primarily top-down	Messages are broadcast to employees	Top executives create and control messaging	Communication is fragmented, reactive, and ad hoc
Tone is formal and corporate	Print newsletters, memos, and speeches predominate	Employees are passive consumers of information	Leaders use assertion to achieve strategic alignment
New model: organizational communication			
Communication is personal and direct	Leaders talk *with* employees, not to them	Leaders relinquish a measure of control over content	A clear agenda informs all communication
Leaders value trust and authenticity	Organizational culture fosters back-and-forth, face-to-face interaction	Employees actively participate in organizational messaging	Leaders carefully explain the agenda to employees
			Strategy emerges from a cross-organizational conversation
What it means for employers and employees			
Leaders emphasize listening to employees rather than just speaking to them	Leaders use video and social media tools to facilitate two-way communication	Leaders involve employees in telling the company story	Leaders build their messaging around company strategy
Employees engage in a bottom-up exchange of ideas	Employees interact with colleagues through blogs and discussion forums	Employees act as brand ambassadors and thought leaders	Employees take part in creating strategy via specially designed communication vehicles

Idea in Brief

One-way, top-down communication between leaders and their employees is no longer useful or even realistic.

Today's leaders achieve far more engagement and credibility when they take part in genuine conversation with the people who work for and with them. A conversation is a frank exchange of ideas and information with an implicit or explicit agenda.

Corporate conversation reflects a new reality: Thanks in part to digital and social technologies, employees have found a public voice. They'll use it whether their bosses like it or not.

The good news for leaders is that people can talk up a company in a way that's more interesting and attractive than any obvious public relations campaign.

Smart leaders today, we have found, engage with employees in a way that resembles an ordinary person-to-person conversation more than it does a series of commands from on high. Furthermore, they initiate practices and foster cultural norms that instill a conversational sensibility throughout their organizations. Chief among the benefits of this approach is that it allows a large or growing company to function like a small one. By talking with employees, rather than simply issuing orders, leaders can retain or recapture some of the qualities—operational flexibility, high levels of employee engagement, tight strategic alignment— that enable start-ups to outperform better-established rivals.

In developing our model, we have identified four elements of organizational conversation that reflect the essential attributes of interpersonal conversation: intimacy, interactivity, inclusion, and intentionality. Leaders who power their organizations through conversation-based practices need not (so to speak) dot all four of these i's. However, as we've discovered in our research, these elements tend to reinforce one another. In the end, they coalesce to form a single integrated process.

Intimacy: Getting Close

Personal conversation flourishes to the degree that the participants stay close to each other, figuratively as well as literally. Organizational conversation, similarly, requires leaders to minimize the

3

distances—institutional, attitudinal, and sometimes spatial—that typically separate them from their employees. Where conversational intimacy prevails, those with decision-making authority seek and earn the trust (and hence the careful attention) of those who work under that authority. They do so by cultivating the art of listening to people at all levels of the organization and by learning to speak with employees directly and authentically. Physical proximity between leaders and employees isn't always feasible. Nor is it essential. What *is* essential is mental or emotional proximity. Conversationally adept leaders step down from their corporate perches and then step up to the challenge of communicating personally and transparently with their people.

This intimacy distinguishes organizational conversation from long-standard forms of corporate communication. It shifts the focus from a top-down distribution of information to a bottom-up exchange of ideas. It's less corporate in tone and more casual. And it's less about issuing and taking orders than about asking and answering questions.

Conversational intimacy can become manifest in various ways— among them gaining trust, listening well, and getting personal.

Gaining trust

Where there is no trust, there can be no intimacy. For all practical purposes, the reverse is true as well. No one will dive into a heart-felt exchange of views with someone who seems to have a hidden agenda or a hostile manner, and any discussion that does unfold between two people will be rewarding and substantive only to the extent that each person can take the other at face value.

But trust is hard to achieve. In organizations it has become especially difficult for employees to put trust in their leaders, who will earn it only if they are authentic and straightforward. That may mean addressing topics that feel off-limits, such as sensitive financial data.

Athenahealth, a medical-records technology provider, has gone as far as to treat every last one of its employees as an "insider" under the strict legal meaning of the term. Insiders are defined as employees entrusted with strategic and financial information that could materially affect the company's business prospects and hence its stock price—a status typically accorded only to top-tier officers. Opening the books to such a degree was a risky move, discouraged by the company's underwriters and frowned upon by the SEC. But Athenahealth's leaders wanted employees to become insiders in more than just the regulatory sense; they wanted them to be thoroughly involved in the business.

Listening well

Leaders who take organizational conversation seriously know when to stop talking and start listening. Few behaviors enhance conversational intimacy as much as attending to what people say. True attentiveness signals respect for people of all ranks and roles, a sense of curiosity, and even a degree of humility.

Duke Energy's president and CEO, James E. Rogers, instituted a series of what he called "listening sessions" when he was the CEO and chairman of Cinergy (which later merged with Duke). Meeting with groups of 90 to 100 managers in three-hour sessions, he invited participants to raise any pressing issues. Through these discussions he gleaned information that might otherwise have escaped his attention. At one session, for example, he heard from a group of supervisors about a problem related to uneven compensation. "You know how long it would have taken for that to bubble up in the organization?" he asks. Having heard directly from those affected by the problem, he could instruct his HR department to find a solution right away.

Getting personal

Rogers not only invited people to raise concerns about the company but also solicited feedback on his own performance. He asked employees at one session to grade him on a scale of A to F. The results, recorded anonymously, immediately appeared on a screen for all to see. The grades were generally good, but less than half of employees were willing to give him an A. He took the feedback seriously and began to conduct the exercise regularly. He also began asking open-ended questions about his performance. Somewhat ironically, he found that "internal communication" was the area in which the highest number of participants believed he had room for improvement. Even as Rogers sought to get close to employees by way of organizational conversation, a fifth of his people were urging him to get closer still. True listening involves taking the bad with the good, absorbing criticism even when it is direct and personal—and even when those delivering it work for you.

At Exelon, an energy provider headquartered in Chicago, a deeply personal form of organizational conversation emerged from a project aimed at bringing the company's corporate values alive for its employees. Values statements typically do little to instill intimacy; they're generally dismissed as just talk. So Exelon experimented in its communication about diversity, a core value: It used a series of short video clips—no fuss, no pretense, no high production values—of top leaders speaking unscripted, very personally, about what diversity meant to them. They talked about race, sexual orientation, and other issues that rarely go on the table in a corporation. Ian McLean, then an Exelon finance executive, spoke of growing up in Manchester, England, the son of a working-class family, and feeling the sting of class prejudice. Responding to a question about a time when he felt "different," he described going to work in a bank where most of his colleagues had upper-class backgrounds: "My accent was different. . . . I wasn't included, I wasn't invited, and I was made to think I wasn't quite as smart as they were. . . . I never want anyone else to feel that [way] around me." Such unadorned stories make a strong impression on employees.

Interactivity: Promoting Dialogue

A personal conversation, by definition, involves an exchange of comments and questions between two or more people. The sound of one person talking is not, obviously, a conversation. The same applies to organizational conversation, in which leaders talk *with* employees and not just *to* them. This interactivity makes the conversation open and fluid rather than closed and directive. It entails shunning the simplicity of monologue and embracing

The New Realities of Leadership Communication

FIVE LONG-TERM BUSINESS TRENDS are forcing the shift from corporate communication to organizational conversation.

Economic Change

As service industries have become more economically significant than manufacturing industries, and as knowledge work has supplanted other kinds of labor, the need for sophisticated ways to process and share information has grown more acute.

Organizational Change

As companies have become flatter and less hierarchical, and frontline employees more pivotally involved in value-creating work, lateral and bottom-up communication has achieved the importance of top-down communication.

Global Change

As workforces have become more diverse and more widely dispersed, navigating across cultural and geographic lines has required interactions that are fluid and complex.

Generational Change

As millennials and other younger workers have gained a foothold in organizations, they have expected peers and authority figures alike to communicate with them in a dynamic, two-way fashion.

Technological Change

As digital networks have made instant connectivity a norm of business life, and as social media platforms have grown more powerful and more ubiquitous, a reliance on older, less conversational channels of communication has ceased to be tenable.

---

the unpredictable vitality of dialogue. The pursuit of interactivity reinforces, and builds upon, intimacy: Efforts to close gaps between employees and their leaders will founder if employees don't have both the tools and the institutional support they need to speak up and (where appropriate) talk back.

In part, a shift toward greater interactivity reflects a shift in the use of communication channels. For decades, technology made it difficult or impossible to support interaction within organizations of any appreciable size. The media that companies used to achieve scale and efficiency in their communications—print and broadcast, in particular—operated in one direction only. But new channels have disrupted that one-way structure. Social technology gives leaders and their employees the ability to invest an organizational setting with the style and spirit of personal conversation.

Yet interactivity isn't just a matter of finding and deploying the right technology. Equally if not more important is the need to buttress social media with social *thinking*. Too often, an organization's prevailing culture works against any attempt to transform corporate communication into a two-way affair. For many executives and managers, the temptation to treat every medium at their disposal as if it were a megaphone has proved hard to resist. In some companies, however, leaders have fostered a genuinely interactive culture—values, norms, and behaviors that create a welcoming space for dialogue.

To see how interactivity works, consider Cisco Systems. As it happens, Cisco makes and sells various products that fall under the social technology umbrella. In using them internally, its people have explored the benefits of enabling high-quality back-and-forth communication. One such product, TelePresence, simulates an in-person meeting by beaming video feeds between locations. Multiple large screens create a wraparound effect, and specially designed meeting tables (in an ideal configuration) mirror one another so that users feel as if they were seated at the same piece of furniture. In one sense this is a more robust version of a web-based video chat, with none of the delays or hiccups that typically mar online video. More important, it masters the critical issue of visual scale. When Cisco engineers studied remote interactions, they found that if the on-screen image of a person is less than 80% of his or her true size, those who see the image are less engaged in talking with that person. TelePresence participants appear life-size and can look one another in the eye.

TelePresence is a sophisticated technology tool, but what it enables is the recovery of immediate, spontaneous give-and-take.

Randy Pond, Cisco's executive vice president of operations, processes, and systems, thinks this type of interaction offers the benefit of the "whole" conversation—a concept he illustrated for us with an anecdote. Sitting at his desk for a video conference one day, he could see video feeds of several colleagues on his computer screen when he made a comment to the group and a participant "just put his head in his hands"—presumably in dismay, and presumably not considering that Pond could see him. "I said, 'I can see you,'" Pond told us. "'If you disagree, *tell me.*'" Pond was then able to engage with his skeptical colleague to get the "whole story." A less interactive form of communication might have produced such information eventually—but far less efficiently.

At the crux of Cisco's communication culture is its CEO, John Chambers, who holds various forums to keep in touch with employees. About every other month, for instance, he leads a "birthday chat," open to any Cisco employee whose birthday falls in the relevant two-month period. Senior managers aren't invited, lest their presence keep attendees from speaking openly. Chambers also records a video blog about once a month—a brief, improvisational message delivered by e-mail to all employees. The use of video allows him to speak to his people directly, informally, and without a script; it suggests immediacy and builds trust. And despite the inherently one-way nature of a video blog, Chambers and his team have made it interactive by inviting video messages as well as text comments from employees.

Inclusion: Expanding Employees' Roles

At its best, personal conversation is an equal-opportunity endeavor. It enables participants to share ownership of the substance of their discussion. As a consequence, they can put their own ideas—and, indeed, their hearts and souls—into the conversational arena. Organizational conversation, by the same token, calls on employees to participate in generating the content that makes up a company's story. Inclusive leaders, by counting employees among a company's official or quasi-official communicators, turn those employees into full-fledged conversation partners. In the process, such leaders raise the level of emotional engagement that employees bring to company life in general.

Inclusion adds a critical dimension to the elements of intimacy and interactivity. Whereas intimacy involves the efforts of leaders to get closer to employees, inclusion focuses on the role that employees play in that process. It also extends the practice of interactivity by enabling employees to provide their own ideas—often on official company channels—rather than simply parrying the ideas that others present. It enables them to serve as frontline *content providers*.

In the standard corporate communication model, top executives and professional communicators monopolize the creation of content and keep a tight rein on what people write or say on official company channels. But when a spirit of inclusion takes hold, engaged employees can adopt important new roles, creating content themselves and acting as brand ambassadors, thought leaders, and storytellers.

Brand ambassadors

When employees feel passionate about their company's products and services, they become living representatives of the brand. This can and does happen organically—lots of people love what they do for a living and will talk it up on their own time. But some companies actively promote that kind of behavior. Coca-Cola, for instance, has created a formal ambassadorship program, aimed at encouraging employees to promote the Coke image and product line in speech and in practice. The Coke intranet provides resources such as a tool that connects employees to company-sponsored volunteer activities. The centerpiece of the program is a list of nine ambassadorial behaviors, which include helping the company "win at the point of sale" (by taking it on themselves to tidy store displays in retail outlets, for example), relaying sales leads, and reporting instances in which a retailer has run out of a Coke product.

Thought leaders

To achieve market leadership in a knowledge-based field, companies may rely on consultants or in-house professionals to draft speeches, articles, white papers, and the like. But often the most innovative thinking occurs deep within an organization, where people develop and test new products and services. Empowering those people to create and promote thought-leadership material can be a smart, quick way to bolster a company's reputation among key industry players. In recent years Juniper Networks has sponsored initiatives to get potential thought leaders out of their labs and offices and into public venues where industry experts and customers can watch them strut their intellectual stuff. The company's engineers are working on the next wave of systems silicon and hardware and can offer keen insights into trends. To communicate their perspective to relevant audiences, Juniper dispatches them to national and international technology conferences and arranges for them to meet with customers at company-run briefing centers.

Storytellers
People are accustomed to hearing corporate communication professionals tell stories about a company, but there's nothing like hearing a story direct from the front lines. When employees speak from their own experience, unedited, the message comes to life. The computer storage giant EMC actively elicits stories from its people. Leaders look to them for ideas on how to improve business performance and for thoughts about the company itself. The point is to instill the notion that ideas are welcome from all corners. As just one example, in 2009 the company published *The Working Mother Experience*—a 250-page coffee-table book written by and for EMCers on the topic of being both a successful EMC employee and a parent. The project, initiated at the front lines, was championed by Frank Hauck, then the executive vice president of global marketing and customer quality. It's not unusual for a big company like EMC to produce such a book as a vanity project, but this was no corporate communication effort; it was a peer-driven endeavor, led by employees. Several dozen EMCers also write blogs, many on public sites, expressing their unfiltered thoughts about life at the company and sharing their ideas about technology.

Of course, inclusion means that executives cede a fair amount of control over how the company is represented to the world. But the fact is that cultural and technological changes have eroded that control anyway. Whether you like it or not, anybody can tarnish (or polish) your company's reputation right from her cube, merely by e-mailing an internal document to a reporter, a blogger, or even a group of friends—or by posting her thoughts in an online forum. Thus inclusive leaders are making a virtue out of necessity. Scott Huennekens, the CEO of Volcano Corporation, suggests that a looser approach to communication has made organizational life less stifling and more productive than it used to be. The free flow of information creates a freer spirit. Some companies do try to set some basic expectations. Infosys, for instance, acknowledging its lack of control over employees' participation in social networks, tells employees that they may disagree but asks them not to be *disagreeable*.

And quite often, leaders have discovered, a system of self-regulation by employees fills the void left by top-down control. Somebody comes out with an outrageous statement, the community responds, and the overall sentiment swings back to the middle.

Intentionality: Pursuing an Agenda

A personal conversation, if it's truly rich and rewarding, will be open but not aimless; the participants will have some sense of what they hope to achieve. They might seek to entertain each other, or to persuade each other, or to learn from each other. In the absence of such intent, a conversation will either meander or run into a blind alley. Intent confers order and meaning on even the loosest and most digressive forms of chatter. That principle applies to organizational conversation, too. Over time, the many voices that contribute to the process of communication within a company must converge on a single vision of what that communication is *for*. To put it another way: The conversation that unfolds within a company should reflect a shared agenda that aligns with the company's strategic objectives.

Intentionality differs from the other three elements of organizational conversation in one key respect. While intimacy, interactivity, and inclusion all serve to open up the flow of information and ideas within a company, intentionality brings a measure of closure to that process: It enables leaders and employees to derive strategically relevant action from the push and pull of discussion and debate. Conversational intentionality requires leaders to convey strategic principles not just by asserting them but by explaining them— by generating consent rather than commanding assent. In this new model, leaders speak extensively and explicitly with employees about the vision and the logic that underlie executive decision making. As a result, people at every level gain a big-picture view of where their company stands within its competitive environment. In short, they become *conversant* in matters of organizational strategy.

One way to help employees understand the company's governing strategy is to let them have a part in creating it. The leadership team at Infosys has taken to including a broad range of employees in the company's annual strategy-development process. In late 2009, as Infosys leaders began to build an organizational strategy for the 2011 fiscal year, they invited people from every rank and division of the company to join in. In particular, explains Kris Gopalakrishnan, a cofounder and executive cochairman, they asked employees to submit ideas on "the significant transformational trends that we see affecting our customers." Using those ideas, strategic planners at Infosys came up with a list of 17 trends, ranging from the growth of emerging markets to the increasing emphasis on environmental sustainability. They then created a series of online forums in which employees could suggest how to match each trend with various customer solutions that the company might offer. Technology and social networks enabled bottom-up participation across the company.

In 2008 Kingfisher plc, the world's third-largest home improvement retailer, began pursuing a new strategy to transform a group of historically discrete business units into "one team," in part through intentional organizational conversation. To launch the effort, company leaders held a three-day event in Barcelona for retail executives. On the second day everyone participated in a 90-minute session called Share at the Marketplace, which was intended to emulate a classic Mediterranean or Middle Eastern bazaar. One group of participants, called "suppliers," donned aprons, and each person stood at one of 22 stalls, ready to give a spiel about a business practice developed by people in his or her part of the Kingfisher organization. Essentially they were purveyors of ideas.

Another group—executive committee members—served as facilitators, ambling through the aisles and providing words of encouragement. The third and largest group acted as buyers, moving from one stall to the next, examining the "merchandise," and occasionally "purchasing" one of the ideas. Using special checkbooks issued for this purpose, buyers could draft up to five checks each to pay for suppliers' wares. Such transactions had no force beyond the confines of the session, but they conveyed a strong message to the suppliers: What you're telling me is impressive. The essence of the marketplace was the peer-to-peer sharing of best practices in an informal, messy, and noisy environment. But the idea was also to treat conversation as a means to an end—to use it to achieve strategic alignment across a diverse group of participants.

Conversation goes on in every company, whether you recognize it or not. That has always been the case, but today the conversation has the potential to spread well beyond your walls, and it's largely out of your control. Smart leaders find ways to use conversation—to manage the flow of information in an honest, open fashion. One-way broadcast messaging is a relic, and slick marketing materials have as little effect on employees as they do on customers. But people will listen to communication that is intimate, interactive, inclusive, and intentional.

Originally published in June 2012. Reprint R1206D

How Managers Become Leaders

The Seven Seismic Shifts of Perspective and Responsibility. *by Michael D. Watkins*

HARALD (NOT HIS REAL NAME) is a high-potential leader with 15 years of experience at a leading European chemical company. He started as an assistant product manager in the plastics unit and was quickly transferred to Hong Kong to help set up the unit's new Asian business center. As sales there soared, he soon won a promotion to sales manager. Three years later he returned to Europe as the marketing and sales director for Europe, the Middle East, and Africa, overseeing a group of 80 professionals. Continuing his string of successes, he was promoted to vice president of marketing and sales for the polyethylene division, responsible for several lines of products, related services, and a staff of nearly 200.

All of Harald's hard work culminated in his appointment as the head of the company's plastic resins unit, a business with more than 3,000 employees worldwide. Quite intentionally, the company had assigned him to run a small but thriving business with a strong team. The idea was to give him the opportunity to move beyond managing sales and marketing, get his arms around an entire business, learn what it meant to head up a unit with the help of his more-experienced team, and take his leadership skills to the next level in a situation free from complicating problems or crises. The setup seemed perfect, but a few months into the new position, Harald was struggling mightily.

Like Harald, many rising stars trip when they shift from leading a function to leading an enterprise and for the first time taking responsibility for a P&L and oversight of executives across corporate functions. It truly is different at the top. To find out how, I took an in-depth look at this critical turning point, conducting an extensive series of interviews with more than 40 executives, including managers who had developed high-potential talent, senior HR professionals, and individuals who had recently made the move to enterprise leadership for the first time.

What I found is that to make the transition successfully, executives must navigate a tricky set of changes in their leadership focus and skills, which I call the seven seismic shifts. They must learn to move from specialist to generalist, analyst to integrator, tactician to strategist, bricklayer to architect, problem solver to agenda setter, warrior to diplomat, and supporting cast member to lead role. Like so many of his peers, Harald had trouble negotiating most of these shifts. To see what makes them so difficult, let's follow him through each of them, as he confronts unnerving surprises, makes unwarranted assumptions, encounters entirely new demands on his time and imagination, makes decisions in ignorance, and learns from his mistakes.

Specialist to Generalist

Harald's immediate challenge was shifting from leading a single function to overseeing the full set of business functions. In his first couple of months, this shift left him feeling disoriented and less confident in his ability to make good judgments. And so he fell into a classic trap—overmanaging the function he knew well and undermanaging the others. Fortunately for Harald, this became crystal clear when his vice president of HR gave him some blunt feedback about his relationship with his sales and marketing VP: "You are driving Claire crazy. You need to give her some space."

Harald's tendency to stay in his functional comfort zone is an understandable reaction to the stresses of moving up to a much broader role. It would be wonderful if newly appointed enterprise leaders

Idea in Brief

Few leadership transitions are as challenging as the move from running a function to running an entire enterprise for the first time.

The scope and complexity of the job dramatically increase in ways that can leave newly minted unit heads feeling overwhelmed and uncertain. The skills that they've honed in their previous roles—mastery of their function, organizational know-how, the ability to build and motivate a team—are no longer enough. For the first time, these executives must transform themselves into generalists who understand all the functions. They

must learn to hire, judge, and mediate with a far wider variety of people. They must confront a whole new range of tough questions: What are the big issues on our corporate agenda? What opportunities and threats does the whole business face? How can I ensure the success of the entire organization?

At this critical turning point, executives must undergo seven seismic shifts—a tricky set of changes in their leadership focus that require them to develop new skills and conceptual frameworks.

were world-class experts in all business functions, but of course they never are. In some instances they have gained experience by rotating through various functions or working on cross-functional projects, which certainly helps. (See the sidebar "How to Develop Strong Enterprise Leaders.") But the reality is that the move to enterprise leadership always requires executives who've been specialists to quickly turn into generalists who know enough about all the functions to run their businesses.

What is "enough"? Enterprise leaders must be able to (1) make decisions that are good for the business as a whole and (2) evaluate the talent on their teams. To do both they need to recognize that business functions are distinct managerial subcultures, each with its own mental models and language. Effective leaders understand the different ways that professionals in finance, marketing, operations, HR, and R&D approach business problems, and the various tools (discounted cash flow, customer segmentation, process flow, succession planning, stage gates, and the like) that each discipline applies. Leaders must be able to speak the language of all the functions and translate for them when necessary. And critically, leaders must

The Seven Seismic Shifts

ALL THE SHIFTS A FUNCTION head must make when first becoming an enterprise leader involve learning new skills and cultivating new mindsets. Here are the shifts and what each requires executives to do:

Specialist to Generalist

Understand the mental models, tools, and terms used in key business functions and develop templates for evaluating the leaders of those functions.

Analyst to Integrator

Integrate the collective knowledge of cross-functional teams and make appropriate trade-offs to solve complex organizational problems.

Tactician to Strategist

Shift fluidly between the details and the larger picture, perceive important patterns in complex environments, and anticipate and influence the reactions of key external players.

Bricklayer to Architect

Understand how to analyze and design organizational systems so that strategy, structure, operating models, and skill bases fit together effectively and

---

know the right questions to ask and the right metrics for evaluating and recruiting people to manage areas in which they themselves are not experts.

The good news for Harald was that, in addition to assigning him to a high-performing unit, his company had strong systems in place for evaluating and developing talent in key functions. These included well-crafted systems for performance reviews and 360-degree feedback, and for collecting input from corporate functions. His heads of finance and HR, for instance, while reporting directly to him, also had dotted-line reporting relationships with their respective corporate departments, which assisted Harald with their evaluation and development. So he had plenty of resources to help him understand what "excellence" meant for each function.

efficiently, and harness this understanding to make needed organizational changes.

Problem Solver to Agenda Setter

Define the problems the organization should focus on, and spot issues that don't fall neatly into any one function but are still important.

Warrior to Diplomat

Proactively shape the environment in which the business operates by influencing key external constituencies, including the government, NGOs, the media, and investors.

Supporting Cast Member to Lead Role

Exhibit the right behaviors as a role model for the organization and learn to communicate with and inspire large groups of people both directly and, increasingly, indirectly.

By investing directly in creating standardized evaluation schemes for each function, companies can ensure that new enterprise leaders get the lay of the land faster. But even if their firms don't have such systems, aspiring enterprise leaders can prepare themselves by building relationships with colleagues in other functions, seeking to learn from them (perhaps in exchange for insight into their own functions) so that they can develop their own templates.

Analyst to Integrator

The primary responsibility of functional leaders is to recruit, develop, and manage people who focus in analytical depth on specific business activities. An enterprise leader's job is to manage and integrate the collective knowledge of those functional teams to solve important organizational problems.

Harald found himself struggling with this shift early on as he sought to address the many competing demands of the business. His sales and marketing VP, for example, wanted to aggressively go to market with a new product, while his head of operations worried that production couldn't be ramped up quickly enough to meet the sales staff's demand scenarios. Harald's team expected him to balance the needs of the supply side of the business (operations) with those of its demand side (sales and marketing), to know when to focus on the quarterly business results (finance) and when to invest in the future (R&D), to decide how much attention to devote to execution and how much to innovation, and to make many other such calls.

Once again, executives need general knowledge of the various functions to resolve such competing issues, but that isn't enough. The skills required have less to do with analysis and more to do with understanding how to make trade-offs and explain the rationale for those decisions. Here, too, previous experience with cross-functional or new-product development teams would stand newly minted enterprise leaders in good stead, as would a previous apprenticeship as a chief of staff to a senior executive. But ultimately, as Harald found, there is no substitute for actually making the calls and learning from their outcome.

Tactician to Strategist

In his early months, Harald threw himself into the myriad details of the business. Being tactical was seductive—the activities were so concrete and the results so immediate. Consequently, he lost himself in the day-to-day flow of attending meetings, making decisions, and pushing projects forward.

The problem with this, of course, was that a core part of Harald's new role was to be strategist-in-chief for the unit he now led. To do that, he had to let go of many of the details and free his mind and his time to focus on higher-level matters. More generally, he needed to adopt a strategic mind-set.

How do tactically strong leaders learn to develop such a mind-set? By cultivating three skills: level shifting, pattern recognition, and mental simulation. *Level shifting* is the ability to move fluidly among levels of analysis—to know when to focus on the details, when to focus on the big picture, and how the two relate. *Pattern recognition* is the ability to discern important causal relationships and other significant patterns in a complex business and its environment—that is, to separate the signal from the noise. *Mental simulation* is the ability to anticipate how outside parties (competitors, regulators, the media, key members of the public) will respond to what you do, to predict their actions and reactions in order to define the best course to take. In Harald's first year, for instance, an Asian competitor introduced a lower-cost substitute for a key resin product his unit made. Harald needed not only to consider the immediate threat but also to think expansively about what the competitor's future intentions might be. Was the Asian company going to use this low-end product to forge strong customer relationships and progressively offer a broader range of products? If so, what options should Harald's unit pursue? How would the competitor respond to what Harald chose to do? Those were not questions he had been responsible for as head of marketing and sales. In the end, after analyzing various courses of action with his senior team, he chose to lower prices, forgoing some current profits in an effort to slow the loss of market share—a move he did not live to regret.

Are strategic thinkers born or made? The answer is both. There's no doubt that strategic thinking, like any other skill, can be improved with training. But the ability to shift through different levels of analysis, recognize patterns, and construct mental models requires some natural propensity. One of the paradoxes of leadership development is that people earn promotions to senior functional levels predominantly by being good at blocking and tackling, but employees with strategic talent may struggle at lower levels because they focus less on the details. Darwinian forces can winnow strategic thinkers out of the developmental pipeline too soon if companies don't adopt explicit policies to identify and to some degree protect them in their early careers.

How to Develop Strong Enterprise Leaders

Early in their careers, give potential leaders . . .

- Experience on cross-functional projects and then responsibility for them
- An international assignment (if it's a global business)
- Exposure to a broad range of business situations: startup, accelerated growth, sustaining success, realignment, turnaround, and shutdown

When their leadership promise becomes evident, give high potentials . . .

- A position on a senior management team
- Experience with external stakeholders (investors, the media, key customers)
- An assignment as chief of staff for an experienced enterprise leader

Bricklayer to Architect

Too often, senior executives dabble in the profession of organizational design without a license—and end up committing malpractice. They come into their first enterprise-level role itching to make their mark and then target elements of the organization that seem relatively easy to change, like strategy or structure, without completely understanding the effect their moves will have on the organization as a whole.

About four months into his new role, for example, Harald concluded that he needed to restructure the business to focus more on customers and less on product lines. It was natural for him, as a former head of sales and marketing, to think this way. In his eyes it was obvious that the business was too rooted in product development and operations and that its structure was an outdated legacy of the way the unit had been founded and grown. So he was surprised when his restructuring proposal was met first with stunned silence from his team and then with vociferous opposition. It rapidly became clear that the existing structure in this successful division was linked in intricate and nonobvious ways to its key processes

- An appointment to lead an acquisition integration or a substantial restructuring

Some time just before their first enterprise promotion, send rising stars . . .

- To a substantial executive program that addresses such capabilities as organizational design, business process improvement, and transition management, and allows them to build external networks

At the time of their first enterprise-level promotion, place new enterprise leaders in units that are . . .

- Small, distinct, and thriving

- Staffed with an experienced and assertive team that they can learn from

and talent bases. To sell the company's chemicals, for instance, the salespeople needed to have deep product knowledge and the ability to consult with customers on applications. A shift to a customer-focused approach would have required them to sell a broader range of complex products and acquire huge amounts of new expertise. So while a move to a customer-focused structure had potential benefits, certain trade-offs needed to be evaluated. Implementation would, for instance, require significant adjustments to processes and substantial investments in employee retraining. These changes demanded a great deal of thought and analysis.

As leaders move up to the enterprise level, they become responsible for designing and altering the architecture of their organization—its strategy, structure, processes, and skill bases. To be effective organizational architects, they need to think in terms of systems. They must understand how the key elements of the organization fit together and not naively believe, as Harald once did, that they can alter one element without thinking through the implications for all the others. Harald learned this the hard way because nothing in his experience as a functional leader had afforded him the opportunity to think about an organization as a system. Nor did he have enough experience with large-scale organizational change to develop those insights from observation.

In this Harald was typical: Enterprise leaders need to know the principles of organizational change and change management, including the mechanics of organizational design, business process improvement, and transition management. Yet few rising executives get any formal training in these domains, leaving most of them ill equipped to be the architects of their organizations—or even to be educated consumers of the work of organizational development professionals. Here Harald was once again fortunate in having—and having the sense to rely on—an experienced staff that offered him cogent advice about the many interdependencies he had not originally considered. Not all new enterprise leaders are that lucky, of course. But if their companies have invested in sending them to executive education programs that teach organizational change, they'll be better prepared for this shift.

Problem Solver to Agenda Setter

Many managers are promoted to senior levels on the strength of their ability to fix problems. When they become enterprise leaders, however, they must focus less on solving problems and more on defining which problems the organization should be tackling.

To do that, Harald had to perceive the full range of opportunities and threats facing his business, and focus the attention of his team on only the most important ones. He also had to identify the "white spaces"—issues that don't fall neatly into any one function but are still important to the business, such as diversity.

The number of concerns Harald now had to consider was head-spinning. When he had run sales and marketing, he had gained some appreciation for how difficult it was for business heads to prioritize all the issues thrown at them in any given day, week, or month. Still, he was surprised by the scope and complexity of some of the problems at this level. He wasn't sure how to allocate his time and immediately felt overloaded. He knew he needed to delegate more, but he wasn't clear yet about which tasks and assignments he could safely leave to others.

How Do I Evaluate a Sales Executive?

ENTERPRISE LEADERS NEED TO EVALUATE the work of all their functional executives, not just those in the same area they came from. A simple template that systematically lists the most important metrics to track for a particular function, as well as which ones indicate trouble is brewing, will help new leaders get up to speed. Here is an example of a template for sales:

Core Performance Metrics

- Sales of key products versus competitors' key products
- Market share growth in key products
- Execution against business plan commitments

People Management Metrics

- Vacancy rate by region or district
- Rate of internal promotions and strength of internal succession pipeline
- Number of regrettable employee losses and the reasons for them
- Success in recruiting and selection

Customer Metrics

- Customer satisfaction and retention rates
- Evidence of understanding purchasing patterns
- Average amount of sales person interaction with customers

Warning Signs

- Regrettable losses of sales personnel
- Flattening or declining sales
- Lack of internal development for future sales leaders
- Internal promotions with poor results
- Inability to communicate product advantages and disadvantages
- Poor assessment of the organization's strengths and weaknesses
- Lack of time in the field or interactions with customers
- Lack of partnering skills with marketing and other key functions

The skills he had honed as a functional leader—mastery of sales and marketing tools and techniques, organizational know-how, and even the ability to mobilize talent and promote teamwork—were not enough. To work out which problems his team should focus on— that is, to set the agenda—he had to learn to navigate a far more uncertain and ambiguous environment than he was used to. He also needed to learn to communicate priorities in ways his organization could respond to. Given his sales and marketing background, Harald struggled less with how to communicate his agenda. The challenge was figuring out what that agenda was. To some degree he just had to learn from experience, but here again he was aided by the members of his team, who pressed him for guidance on issues they knew he needed to consider. He also could rely on the company's annual planning process, which provided a structure for defining key goals for his unit.

Warrior to Diplomat

In his previous roles, Harald had focused primarily on marshaling the troops to defeat the competition. Now he found himself devoting a surprising amount of time to influencing a host of external constituencies, including regulators, the media, investors, and NGOs. His support staff was bombarded with requests for his time: Could he participate in industry or government forums sponsored by the government affairs department? Would he be willing to sit for an interview with an editor from a leading business publication? Could he meet with a key group of institutional investors? Some of these groups he was familiar with; others not at all. But what was entirely new to him was his responsibility not just to interact with various stakeholders but also to proactively address their concerns in ways that meshed with the firm's interests. Little of Harald's previous experience prepared him for the challenges of being a corporate diplomat.

What do effective corporate diplomats do? They use the tools of diplomacy—negotiation, persuasion, conflict management, and alliance building—to shape the external business environment to support their strategic objectives. In the process they often find themselves collaborating with people with whom they compete aggressively in the market every day.

To do this well, enterprise leaders need to embrace a new mind-set—to look for ways that interests can or do align, understand how decisions are made in different kinds of organizations, and develop effective strategies for influencing others. They must also understand how to recruit and manage employees of a kind that they have probably never supervised before: professionals in key supporting functions such as government relations and corporate communications. And they must recognize that these employees' initiatives have longer horizons than the ongoing business, with its focus on quarterly or even annual results, does. Initiatives like a campaign to shape the development of government regulation can take years to unfold. It took Harald a while to understand this, as his staffers educated him about how painstakingly they managed issues over protracted periods of time and how they periodically bemoaned the results when someone took his eye off the ball.

Supporting Cast Member to Lead Role

Finally, becoming an enterprise leader means moving to center stage under the bright lights. The intensity of the attention and the almost constant need to keep up his guard caught Harald by surprise. He was somewhat shocked to discover how much stock people placed in what he said and did. Not long after he first took the job, for example, he met with his vice president of R&D and mused about a new way of packaging an existing product. Two weeks later a preliminary feasibility report for it appeared on his desk.

In part, this shift is about having a much greater impact as a role model. Managers at all levels are role models to some degree. But at the enterprise level, their influence is magnified, as everyone looks to them for vision, inspiration, and cues about the "right" behaviors and attitudes. For good or ill, the personal styles and quirks of senior leaders are infectious, whether they are observed directly by employees or indirectly transmitted from their reports to the level below and on down through the organization. This effect can't really be avoided, but enterprise leaders can make it less inadvertent by cultivating more self-awareness and taking the time to develop empathy with subordinates' viewpoints. After all, it wasn't so long ago that they were the subordinates, drawing these kinds of inferences from their own bosses' behavior.

Then there is the question of what it means, practically speaking, to lead large groups of people—how to define a compelling vision and share it in an inspiring way. Harald, already a strong communicator who was used to selling ideas along with products, still needed to adjust his thinking in this regard (though perhaps less so than some of his counterparts). In his previous job he had maintained a reasonable degree of personal, albeit sometimes sporadic, contact with most of his employees. Now that he was overseeing 3,000-plus people scattered around the globe, that was simply impossible.

The implications of this became clear as he worked with his team to craft the annual strategy. When the time came to communicate it to the organization, he realized that he couldn't simply go out and sell it himself; he had to work more through his direct reports and find other channels, such as video, for spreading the word. And after touring most of the unit's facilities, Harald likewise worried that he'd never really be able to figure out what was happening on the front lines. So rather than meet just with leaders when he made site visits, he instituted brown-bag lunches with small groups of frontline employees and tuned in to online discussion groups in which employees could comment on the company.

For the most part, the seven shifts involve switching from left-brain, analytical thinking to right-brain conceptual mind-sets. But that doesn't mean enterprise leaders never spend time on tactics or on functional concerns. It's just that they spend far, far less time on those responsibilities than they used to in their previous roles. In fact, it's often helpful for enterprise leaders to engage someone else—a chief of staff, a chief operating officer, or a project manager—to focus on execution, as a way to free up time for their new role.

As for Harald, his story ended well. He was fortunate to be working for a company that believed in leadership development and to have an experienced team that was able—and willing—to give him effective counsel. So despite the many bumps in the road, the business continued to thrive, and Harald eventually found his stride as an enterprise leader. Three years later, armed with all this experience, he was asked to take over a much larger, struggling unit of the company and initiated a successful turn-around. Reflecting back, he says, "The skills that got you where you are may not be the requisite skills to get you to where you need to go. This doesn't discount the accomplishments of your past, but they will not be everything you need for the next leg of the journey."

Originally published in June 2012. Reprint R1206C

Strategic Leadership

The Essential Skills. *by Paul J.H. Schoemaker,*
Steve Krupp, and Samantha Howland

THE STORIED BRITISH BANKER and financier Nathan Rothschild noted that great fortunes are made when cannonballs fall in the harbor, not when violins play in the ballroom. Rothschild understood that the more unpredictable the environment, the greater the opportunity—if you have the leadership skills to capitalize on it. Through research at the Wharton School and at our consulting firm involving more than 20,000 executives to date, we have identified six skills that, when mastered and used in concert, allow leaders to think strategically and navigate the unknown effectively: the abilities to anticipate, challenge, interpret, decide, align, and learn. Each has received attention in the leadership literature, but usually in isolation and seldom in the special context of high stakes and deep uncertainty that can make or break both companies and careers. This article describes the six skills in detail. An adaptive strategic leader—someone who is both resolute and flexible, persistent in the face of setbacks but also able to react strategically to environmental shifts—has learned to apply all six at once.

Do you have the right networks to help you see opportunities before competitors do? Are you comfortable challenging your own and others' assumptions? Can you get a diverse group to buy in to a common vision? Do you learn from mistakes? By answering questions like these, you'll get a clear view of your abilities in each area. The self-test at this article's end (and the more detailed test available online) will help you gauge your strengths and weaknesses, address deficits, and optimize your full portfolio of leadership skills.

Let's look at each skill in turn.

Anticipate

Most organizations and leaders are poor at detecting ambiguous threats and opportunities on the periphery of their business. Coors executives, famously, were late seeing the trend toward low-carb beers. Lego management missed the electronic revolution in toys and gaming. Strategic leaders, in contrast, are constantly vigilant, honing their ability to anticipate by scanning the environment for signals of change.

We worked with a CEO named Mike who had built his reputation as a turnaround wizard in heavy manufacturing businesses. He was terrific at reacting to crises and fixing them. After he'd worked his magic in one particular crisis, Mike's company enjoyed a bump in growth, fueled in part by an up cycle. But after the cycle had peaked, demand abruptly softened, catching Mike off guard. More of the same in a down market wasn't going to work. Mike needed to consider various scenarios and gather better information from diverse sources in order to anticipate where his industry was headed.

We showed Mike and his team members how to pick up weak signals from both inside and outside the organization. They worked to develop broader networks and to take the perspective of customers, competitors, and partners. More alert to opportunities outside the core business, Mike and the team diversified their product portfolio and acquired a company in an adjacent market where demand was higher and less susceptible to boom-and-bust cycles.

To improve your ability to *anticipate*:

- Talk to your customers, suppliers, and other partners to understand their challenges.

- Conduct market research and business simulations to understand competitors' perspectives, gauge their likely reactions

Idea in Brief

The more uncertain your environment, the greater the opportunity—if you have the leadership skills to capitalize on it. Research at the Wharton School and at the authors' consulting firm, involving more than 20,000 executives to date, has identified six skills that, when mastered and used in concert, allow leaders to think strategically and navigate the unknown effectively. They are the abilities to anticipate, challenge, interpret, decide, align, and learn. This article describes the six skills in detail and includes a self-assessment that will enable you to identify the ones that most need your attention. The authors have found that strength in one skill cannot easily compensate for a deficit in another. An adaptive strategic leader has learned to apply all six at once.

to new initiatives or products, and predict potential disruptive offerings.

- Use scenario planning to imagine various futures and prepare for the unexpected.

- Look at a fast-growing rival and examine actions it has taken that puzzle you.

- List customers you have lost recently and try to figure out why.

- Attend conferences and events in other industries or functions.

Challenge

Strategic thinkers question the status quo. They challenge their own and others' assumptions and encourage divergent points of view. Only after careful reflection and examination of a problem through many lenses do they take decisive action. This requires patience, courage, and an open mind.

Consider Bob, a division president in an energy company we worked with, who was set in his ways and avoided risky or messy situations. When faced with a tough problem—for example, how to consolidate business units to streamline costs—he would gather all available information and retreat alone into his office. His solutions, although well thought out, were predictable and rarely innovative. In the consolidation case he focused entirely on two similar and underperforming businesses rather than considering a bolder reorganization that would streamline activities across the entire division. When he needed outside advice, he turned to a few seasoned consultants in one trusted firm who suggested tried-and-true solutions instead of questioning basic industry assumptions.

Through coaching, we helped Bob learn how to invite different (even opposing) views to challenge his own thinking and that of his advisers. This was uncomfortable for him at first, but then he began to see that he could generate fresh solutions to stale problems and improve his strategic decision making. For the organizational streamlining he even assigned a colleague to play devil's advocate—an approach that yielded a hybrid solution: Certain emerging market teams were allowed to keep their local HR and finance support for a transitional period while tapping the fully centralized model for IT and legal support.

To improve your ability to *challenge*:

- Focus on the root causes of a problem rather than the symptoms. Apply the "five whys" of Sakichi Toyoda, Toyota's founder. ("Product returns increased 5% this month." "Why?" "Because the product intermittently malfunctions." "Why?" And so on.)

- List long-standing assumptions about an aspect of your business ("High switching costs prevent our customers from defecting") and ask a diverse group if they hold true.

- Encourage debate by holding "safe zone" meetings where open dialogue and conflict are expected and welcomed.

- Create a rotating position for the express purpose of questioning the status quo.

- Include naysayers in a decision process to surface challenges early.

- Capture input from people not directly affected by a decision who may have a good perspective on the repercussions.

Interpret

Leaders who challenge in the right way invariably elicit complex and conflicting information. That's why the best ones are also able to interpret. Instead of reflexively seeing or hearing what you expect, you should synthesize all the input you have. You'll need to recognize patterns, push through ambiguity, and seek new insights. Finland's former president J. K. Paasikivi was fond of saying that wisdom begins by recognizing the facts and then "re-cognizing," or rethinking, them to expose their hidden implications.

Some years ago Liz, a U.S. food company CMO, was developing a marketing plan for the company's low-carb cake line. At the time, the Atkins diet was popular, and every food company had a low-carb strategy. But Liz noticed that none of the consumers she listened to were avoiding the company's snacks because they were on a low-carb diet. Rather, a fast-growing segment—people with diabetes—shunned them because they contained sugar. Liz thought her company might achieve higher sales if it began to serve diabetics rather than fickle dieters. Her ability to connect the dots ultimately led to a profitable change in product mix from low-carb to sugar-free cakes.

To improve your ability to *interpret*:

- When analyzing ambiguous data, list at least three possible explanations for what you're observing and invite perspectives from diverse stakeholders.

- Force yourself to zoom in on the details and out to see the big picture.

- Actively look for missing information and evidence that disconfirms your hypothesis.

- Supplement observation with quantitative analysis.
- Step away—go for a walk, look at art, put on nontraditional music, play Ping-Pong—to promote an open mind.

Decide

In uncertain times, decision makers may have to make tough calls with incomplete information, and often they must do so quickly. But strategic thinkers insist on multiple options at the outset and don't get prematurely locked into simplistic go/no-go choices. They don't shoot from the hip but follow a disciplined process that balances rigor with speed, considers the trade-offs involved, and takes both short- and long-term goals into account. In the end, strategic leaders must have the courage of their convictions—informed by a robust decision process.

Janet, an execution-oriented division president in a technology business, liked to make decisions quickly and keep the process simple. This worked well when the competitive landscape was familiar and the choices straightforward. Unfortunately for her, the industry was shifting rapidly as nontraditional competitors from Korea began seizing market share with lower-priced products.

Janet's instinct was to make a strategic acquisition in a low-cost geography—a yes-or-no proposition—to preserve the company's competitive pricing position and market share. As the plan's champion, she pushed for a rapid green light, but because capital was short, the CEO and the CFO resisted. Surprised by this, she gathered the principals involved in the decision and challenged them to come up with other options. The team elected to take a methodical approach and explored the possibility of a joint venture or a strategic alliance. On the basis of that analysis, Janet ultimately pursued an acquisition—but of a different company in a more strategic market.

To improve your ability to *decide*:

- Reframe binary decisions by explicitly asking your team, "What other options do we have?"
- Divide big decisions into pieces to understand component parts and better see unintended consequences.

- Tailor your decision criteria to long-term versus short-term projects.

- Let others know where you are in your decision process. Are you still seeking divergent ideas and debate, or are you moving toward closure and choice?

- Determine who needs to be directly involved and who can influence the success of your decision.

- Consider pilots or experiments instead of big bets, and make staged commitments.

Align

Strategic leaders must be adept at finding common ground and achieving buy-in among stakeholders who have disparate views and agendas. This requires active outreach. Success depends on proactive communication, trust building, and frequent engagement.

One executive we worked with, a chemical company president in charge of the Chinese market, was tireless in trying to expand his business. But he had difficulty getting support from colleagues elsewhere in the world. Frustrated that they didn't share his enthusiasm for opportunities in China, he plowed forward alone, further alienating them. A survey revealed that his colleagues didn't fully understand his strategy and thus hesitated to back him.

With our help, the president turned the situation around. He began to have regular face-to-face meetings with his fellow leaders in which he detailed his growth plans and solicited feedback, participation, and differing points of view. Gradually they began to see the benefits for their own functions and lines of business. With greater collaboration, sales increased, and the president came to see his colleagues as strategic partners rather than obstacles.

To improve your ability to *align*:

- Communicate early and often to combat the two most common complaints in organizations: "No one ever asked me" and "No one ever told me."

- Identify key internal and external stakeholders, mapping their positions on your initiative and pinpointing any misalignment of interests. Look for hidden agendas and coalitions.

- Use structured and facilitated conversations to expose areas of misunderstanding or resistance.

- Reach out to resisters directly to understand their concerns and then address them.

- Be vigilant in monitoring stakeholders' positions during the rollout of your initiative or strategy.

- Recognize and otherwise reward colleagues who support team alignment.

Learn

Strategic leaders are the focal point for organizational learning. They promote a culture of inquiry, and they search for the lessons in both successful and unsuccessful outcomes. They study failures—their own and their teams'—in an open, constructive way to find the hidden lessons.

A team of 40 senior leaders from a pharmaceutical company, including the CEO, took our Strategic Aptitude Self-Assessment and discovered that learning was their weakest collective area of leadership. At all levels of the company, it emerged, the tendency was to punish rather than learn from mistakes, which meant that leaders often went to great lengths to cover up their own.

The CEO realized that the culture had to change if the company was to become more innovative. Under his leadership, the team launched three initiatives: (1) a program to publicize stories about projects that initially failed but ultimately led to creative solutions; (2) a program to engage cross-divisional teams in novel experiments to solve customer problems—and then report the results regardless of outcome; (3) an innovation tournament to generate new ideas from across the organization. Meanwhile, the CEO himself became more open in acknowledging his missteps. For example, he described to a group of high potentials how his delay in selling a stalled legacy business unit had prevented the enterprise from acquiring a diagnostics company that would have expanded its market share. The lesson, he explained, was that he should more readily cut losses on underperforming investments. In time the company culture shifted toward more shared learning and bolder innovation.

To improve your ability to *learn*:

- Institute after-action reviews, document lessons learned from major decisions or mile stones (including the termination of a failing project), and broadly communicate the resulting insights.

- Reward managers who try something laudable but fail in terms of outcomes.

- Conduct annual learning audits to see where decisions and team interactions may have fallen short.

- Identify initiatives that are not producing as expected and examine the root causes.

- Create a culture in which inquiry is valued and mistakes are viewed as learning opportunities.

Becoming a strategic leader means identifying weaknesses in the six skills discussed above and correcting them. Our research shows that strength in one skill cannot easily compensate for a deficit in another, so it is important to methodically optimize all six abilities. The following test—a short version of our Strategic Aptitude Assessment, which is available online at hbrsurvey.decisionstrat.com—can help reveal which areas require attention. For clearer and more useful results, take the longer survey and ask colleagues—or at least your manager—to review and comment on your answers.

Are You a Strategic Leader?

AS YOU COMPLETE THIS ASSESSMENT, think about the work you have done over the past year related to developing new strategies, solving business challenges, and making complex decisions. Average your scores for each of the six leadership skills and then address your weakest area first, following the recommendations described in this article and online.

How often do you . . .	Rarely						Almost always
Anticipate				Survey average: 4.99*			
Gather information from a wide network of experts and sources both inside and outside your industry or function.	1	2	3	4	5	6	7
Predict competitors' potential moves and likely reactions to new initiatives or products.	1	2	3	4	5	6	7
Challenge				Survey average: 5.52			
Reframe a problem from several angles to understand root causes.	1	2	3	4	5	6	7
Seek out diverse views to see multiple sides of an issue.	1	2	3	4	5	6	7
Interpret				Survey average: 5.78			
Demonstrate curiosity and an open mind.	1	2	3	4	5	6	7
Test multiple working hypotheses with others before coming to conclusions.	1	2	3	4	5	6	7

Decide   Survey average: 4.81

| Balance long-term investment for growth with short-term pressure for results. | 1 | 2 | 3 | 4 | 5 | 6 | 7 |

| Determine trade-offs, risks, and unintended consequences for customers and other stakeholders when making decisions. | 1 | 2 | 3 | 4 | 5 | 6 | 7 |

Align   Survey average: 5.01

| Assess stakeholders' tolerance and motivation for change. | 1 | 2 | 3 | 4 | 5 | 6 | 7 |

| Pinpoint and address conflicting interests among stakeholders. | 1 | 2 | 3 | 4 | 5 | 6 | 7 |

Learn   Survey average: 4.95

| Communicate stories about success and failure to promote institutional learning. | 1 | 2 | 3 | 4 | 5 | 6 | 7 |

| Course correct on the basis of disconfirming evidence, even after a decision has been made. | 1 | 2 | 3 | 4 | 5 | 6 | 7 |

*Averages are based on responses to this survey from more than 20,000 executives.

Originally published in January–February 2013. Reprint R1301L

The Authenticity Paradox

by Herminia Ibarra

AUTHENTICITY HAS BECOME THE GOLD STANDARD for leadership. But a simplistic understanding of what it means can hinder your growth and limit your impact.

Consider Cynthia, a general manager in a health care organization. Her promotion into that role increased her direct reports 10-fold and expanded the range of businesses she oversaw—and she felt a little shaky about making such a big leap. A strong believer in transparent, collaborative leadership, she bared her soul to her new employees: "I want to do this job," she said, "but it's scary, and I need your help." Her candor backfired; she lost credibility with people who wanted and needed a confident leader to take charge.

Or take George, a Malaysian executive in an auto parts company where people valued a clear chain of command and made decisions by consensus. When a Dutch multinational with a matrix structure acquired the company, George found himself working with peers who saw decision making as a freewheeling contest for the best-debated ideas. That style didn't come easily to him, and it contradicted everything he had learned about humility growing up in his country. In a 360-degree debrief, his boss told him that he needed to sell his ideas and accomplishments more aggressively. George felt he had to choose between being a failure and being a fake.

Because going against our natural inclinations can make us feel like impostors, we tend to latch on to authenticity as an excuse for sticking with what's comfortable. But few jobs allow us to do that for long. That's doubly true when we advance in our careers or when demands or expectations change, as Cynthia, George, and countless other executives have discovered.

In my research on leadership transitions, I have observed that career advances require all of us to move way beyond our comfort zones. At the same time, however, they trigger a strong countervailing impulse to protect our identities: When we are unsure of ourselves or our ability to perform well or measure up in a new setting, we often retreat to familiar behaviors and styles.

But my research also demonstrates that the moments that most challenge our sense of self are the ones that can teach us the most about leading effectively. By viewing ourselves as works in progress and evolving our professional identities through trial and error, we can develop a personal style that feels right to us and suits our organizations' changing needs.

That takes courage, because learning, by definition, starts with unnatural and often superficial behaviors that can make us feel calculating instead of genuine and spontaneous. But the only way to avoid being pigeonholed and ultimately become better leaders is to do the things that a rigidly authentic sense of self would keep us from doing.

Why Leaders Struggle with Authenticity

The word "authentic" traditionally referred to any work of art that is an original, not a copy. When used to describe leadership, of course, it has other meanings—and they can be problematic. For example, the notion of adhering to one "true self" flies in the face of much research on how people evolve with experience, discovering facets of themselves they would never have unearthed through introspection alone. And being utterly transparent—disclosing every single thought and feeling—is both unrealistic and risky.

Idea in Brief

The Problem

When we view authenticity as an unwavering sense of self, we struggle to take on new challenges and bigger roles. The reality is that people learn—and change—who they are through experience.

The Solution

By trying out different leadership styles and behaviors, we grow more than we would through introspection alone. Experimenting with our identities allows us to find the right approach for ourselves and our organizations.

The Sticking Point

This adaptive approach to authenticity can make us feel like impostors, because it involves doing things that may not come naturally. But it's outside our comfort zones that we learn the most about leading effectively.

Leaders today struggle with authenticity for several reasons. First, we make more-frequent and more-radical changes in the kinds of work we do. As we strive to *improve* our game, a clear and firm sense of self is a compass that helps us navigate choices and progress toward our goals. But when we're looking to *change* our game, a too rigid self-concept becomes an anchor that keeps us from sailing forth, as it did at first with Cynthia.

Second, in global business, many of us work with people who don't share our cultural norms and have different expectations for how we should behave. It can often seem as if we have to choose between what is expected—and therefore effective—and what feels authentic. George is a case in point.

Third, identities are always on display in today's world of ubiquitous connectivity and social media. How we present ourselves—not just as executives but as people, with quirks and broader interests—has become an important aspect of leadership. Having to carefully curate a persona that's out there for all to see can clash with our private sense of self.

In dozens of interviews with talented executives facing new expectations, I have found that they most often grapple with authenticity in the following situations.

Taking charge in an unfamiliar role

As everyone knows, the first 90 days are critical in a new leadership role. First impressions form quickly, and they matter. Depending on their personalities, leaders respond very differently to the increased visibility and performance pressure.

Psychologist Mark Snyder, of the University of Minnesota, identified two psychological profiles that inform how leaders develop their personal styles. "High self-monitors"—or chameleons, as I call them—are naturally able and willing to adapt to the demands of a situation without feeling fake. Chameleons care about managing their public image and often mask their vulnerability with bluster. They may not always get it right the first time, but they keep trying on different styles like new clothes until they find a good fit for themselves and their circumstances. Because of that flexibility, they often advance rapidly. But chameleons can run into problems when people perceive them as disingenuous or lacking a moral center—even though they're expressing their "true" chameleon nature.

By contrast, "true-to-selfers" (Snyder's "low self-monitors") tend to express what they really think and feel, even when it runs counter to situational demands. The danger with true-to-selfers like Cynthia and George is that they may stick too long with comfortable behavior that prevents them from meeting new requirements, instead of evolving their style as they gain insight and experience.

Cynthia (whom I interviewed after her story appeared in a *Wall Street Journal* article by Carol Hymowitz) hemmed herself in like this. She thought she was setting herself up for success by staying true to her highly personal, full-disclosure style of management. She asked her new team for support, openly acknowledging that she felt a bit at sea. As she scrambled to learn unfamiliar aspects of the business, she worked tirelessly to contribute to every decision and solve every problem. After a few months, she was on the verge of burnout. To make matters worse, sharing her vulnerability with her team members so early on had damaged her standing. Reflecting on her transition some years later, Cynthia told me: "Being authentic doesn't mean that you can be held up to the light and people can see right through you." But at the time, that was how she saw it—and instead of building trust, she made people question her ability to do the job.

Delegating and communicating appropriately are only part of the problem in a case like this. A deeper-seated issue is finding the right mix of distance and closeness in an unfamiliar situation. Stanford psychologist Deborah Gruenfeld describes this as managing the tension between authority and approachability. To be authoritative, you privilege your knowledge, experience, and expertise over the team's, maintaining a measure of distance. To be approachable, you emphasize your relationships with people, their input, and their perspective, and you lead with empathy and warmth. Getting the balance right presents an acute authenticity crisis for true-to-selfers, who typically have a strong preference for behaving one way or the other. Cynthia made herself too approachable and vulnerable, and it undermined and drained her. In her bigger role, she needed more distance from her employees to gain their confidence and get the job done.

Selling your ideas (and yourself)

Leadership growth usually involves a shift from having good ideas to pitching them to diverse stakeholders. Inexperienced leaders, especially true-to-selfers, often find the process of getting buy-in distasteful because it feels artificial and political; they believe that their work should stand on its own merits.

Here's an example: Anne, a senior manager at a transportation company, had doubled revenue and fundamentally redesigned core processes in her unit. Despite her obvious accomplishments, however, her boss didn't consider her an inspirational leader. Anne also knew she was not communicating effectively in her role as a board member of the parent company. The chairman, a broad-brush thinker, often became impatient with her detail orientation. His feedback to her was "step up, do the vision thing." But to Anne that seemed like valuing form over substance. "For me, it is manipulation," she told me in an interview. "I can do the storytelling too, but I refuse to play on people's emotions. If the string-pulling is too obvious, I can't make myself do it." Like many aspiring leaders, she resisted crafting emotional messages to influence and inspire others because that felt less authentic to her than relying on facts, figures, and spreadsheets. As a result, she worked at cross-purposes with the board chairman, pushing hard on the facts instead of pulling him in as a valued ally.

Many managers know deep down that their good ideas and strong potential will go unnoticed if they don't do a better job of selling themselves. Still, they can't bring themselves to do it. "I try to build a network based on professionalism and what I can deliver for the business, not who I know," one manager told me. "Maybe that's not smart from a career point of view. But I can't go against my beliefs. . . . So I have been more limited in 'networking up.'"

Until we see career advancement as a way of extending our reach and increasing our impact in the organization—a collective win, not just a selfish pursuit—we have trouble feeling authentic when touting our strengths to influential people. True-to-selfers find it particularly hard to sell themselves to senior management when they most need to do so: when they are still unproven. Research shows, however, that this hesitancy disappears as people gain experience and become more certain of the value they bring.

Processing negative feedback

Many successful executives encounter serious negative feedback for the first time in their careers when they take on larger roles or responsibilities. Even when the criticisms aren't exactly new, they loom larger because the stakes are higher. But leaders often convince themselves that dysfunctional aspects of their "natural" style are the inevitable price of being effective.

Let's look at Jacob, a food company production manager whose direct reports gave him low marks in a 360 review on emotional intelligence, team building, and empowering others. One team member wrote that it was hard for Jacob to accept criticism. Another remarked that after an angry outburst, he'd suddenly make a joke as if nothing had happened, not realizing the destabilizing effect of his mood

Why Companies Are Pushing Authenticity Training

MANAGERS CAN CHOOSE from countless books, articles, and executive workshops for advice on how to be more authentic at work. Two trends help explain the exploding popularity of the concept and the training industry it has fed.

First, trust in business leaders fell to an all-time low in 2012, according to the Edelman Trust Barometer. Even in 2013, when trust began to climb back up, only 18% of people reported that they trusted business leaders to tell the truth, and fewer than half trusted businesses to do the right thing.

Second, employee engagement is at a nadir. A 2013 Gallup poll found that only 13% of employees worldwide are engaged at work. Only one in eight workers—out of roughly 180 million employees studied—is psychologically committed to his or her job. In study after study, frustration, burnout, disillusionment, and misalignment with personal values are cited among the biggest reasons for career change.

At a time when public confidence and employee morale are so low, it's no surprise that companies are encouraging leaders to discover their "true" selves.

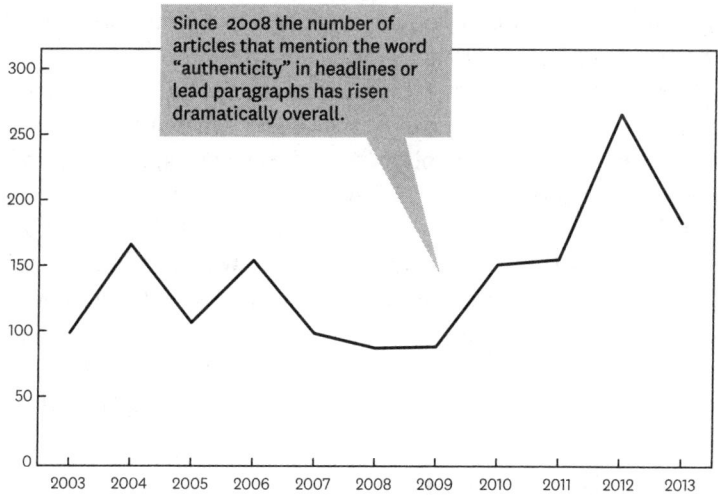

Since 2008 the number of articles that mention the word "authenticity" in headlines or lead paragraphs has risen dramatically overall.

Source: *New York Times, Financial Times, Washington Post, Economist, Forbes, Wall Street Journal,* and *HBR*

changes on those around him. For someone who genuinely believed that he'd built trust among his people, all this was tough to swallow. Once the initial shock had subsided, Jacob acknowledged that this was not the first time he'd received such criticism (some colleagues and subordinates had made similar comments a few years earlier). "I thought I'd changed my approach," he reflected, "but I haven't really changed so much since the last time." However, he quickly rationalized his behavior to his boss: "Sometimes you have to be tough in order to deliver results, and people don't like it," he said. "You have to accept that as part of the job description." Of course, he was missing the point.

Because negative feedback given to leaders often centers on style rather than skills or expertise, it can feel like a threat to their identity—as if they're being asked to give up their "secret sauce." That's how Jacob saw it. Yes, he could be explosive—but from his point of view, his "toughness" allowed him to deliver results year after year. In reality, though, he had succeeded up to this point *despite* his behavior. When his role expanded and he took on greater responsibility, his intense scrutiny of subordinates became an even bigger obstacle because it took up time he should have been devoting to more-strategic pursuits.

A great public example of this phenomenon is Margaret Thatcher. Those who worked with her knew she could be merciless if someone failed to prepare as thoroughly as she did. She was capable of humiliating a staff member in public, she was a notoriously bad listener, and she believed that compromise was cowardice. As she became known to the world as the "Iron Lady," Thatcher grew more and more convinced of the rightness of her ideas and the necessity of her coercive methods. She could beat anyone into submission with the power of her rhetoric and conviction, and she only got better at it. Eventually, though, it was her undoing—she was ousted by her own cabinet.

A Playful Frame of Mind

Such a rigid self-concept can result from too much introspection. When we look only within for answers, we inadvertently reinforce old ways of seeing the world and outdated views of ourselves.

Without the benefit of what I call outsight—the valuable external perspective we get from experimenting with new leadership behaviors—habitual patterns of thought and action fence us in. To begin thinking like leaders, we must first act: plunge ourselves into new projects and activities, interact with very different kinds of people, and experiment with new ways of getting things done. Especially in times of transition and uncertainty, thinking and introspection should follow experience—not vice versa. Action changes who we are and what we believe is worth doing.

Fortunately, there are ways of increasing outsight and evolving toward an "adaptively authentic" way of leading, but they require a playful frame of mind. Think of leadership development as trying on possible selves rather than working on yourself—which, let's face it, sounds like drudgery. When we adopt a playful attitude, we're more open to possibilities. It's OK to be inconsistent from one day to the next. That's not being a fake; it's how we experiment to figure out what's right for the new challenges and circumstances we face.

My research suggests three important ways to get started.

Learn from diverse role models

Most learning necessarily involves some form of imitation—and the understanding that nothing is "original." An important part of growing as a leader is viewing authenticity not as an intrinsic state but as the ability to take elements you have learned from others' styles and behaviors and make them your own.

But don't copy just one person's leadership style; tap many diverse role models. There is a big difference between imitating someone wholesale and borrowing selectively from various people to create your own collage, which you then modify and improve. As the playwright Wilson Mizner said, copying one author is plagiarism, but copying many is research.

I observed the importance of this approach in a study of investment bankers and consultants who were advancing from analytical and project work to roles advising clients and selling new business. Though most of them felt incompetent and insecure in their new positions, the chameleons among them consciously borrowed styles and tactics from successful senior leaders—learning through emulation how to use humor to break tension in meetings, for instance, and how to shape opinion without being overbearing. Essentially, the chameleons faked it until they found what worked for them. Noticing their efforts, their managers provided coaching and mentoring and shared tacit knowledge.

As a result, the chameleons arrived much faster at an authentic but more skillful style than the true-to-selfers in the study, who continued to focus solely on demonstrating technical mastery. Often the true-to-selfers concluded that their managers were "all talk and little content" and therefore not suitable role models. In the absence of a "perfect" model they had a harder time with imitation—it felt bogus. Unfortunately, their managers perceived their inability to adapt as a lack of effort or investment and thus didn't give them as much mentoring and coaching as they gave the chameleons.

Work on getting better

Setting goals for learning (not just for performance) helps us experiment with our identities without feeling like impostors, because we don't expect to get everything right from the start. We stop trying to protect our comfortable old selves from the threats that change can bring, and start exploring what kinds of leaders we might become.

Of course, we all want to perform well in a new situation—get the right strategy in place, execute like crazy, deliver results the organization cares about. But focusing exclusively on those things makes us afraid to take risks in the service of learning. In a series of ingenious experiments, Stanford psychologist Carol Dweck has shown that concern about how we will appear to others inhibits learning on new or unfamiliar tasks. Performance goals motivate us to show others that we possess valued attributes, such as intelligence and social skill, and to prove to ourselves that we have them. By contrast, learning goals motivate us to develop valued attributes.

The Cultural Factor

WHATEVER THE SITUATION—TAKING charge in unfamiliar territory, selling your ideas and yourself, or processing negative feedback—finding authentic ways of being effective is even more difficult in a multicultural environment.

As my INSEAD colleague Erin Meyer finds in her research, styles of persuading others and the kinds of arguments that people find persuasive are far from universal; they are deeply rooted in a culture's philosophical, religious, and educational assumptions. That said, prescriptions for how leaders are supposed to look and sound are rarely as diverse as the leaders themselves. And despite corporate initiatives to build understanding of cultural differences and promote diversity, the fact is that leaders are still expected to express ideas assertively, to claim credit for them, and to use charisma to motivate and inspire people.

Authenticity is supposed to be an antidote to a single model of leadership. (After all, the message is to be yourself, not what someone else expects you to be.) But as the notion has gained currency, it has, ironically, come to mean something much more limiting and culturally specific. A closer look at how leaders are taught to discover and demonstrate authenticity—by telling a personal story about a hardship they have overcome, for example—reveals a model that is, in fact, very American, based on ideals such as self-disclosure, humility, and individualistic triumph over adversity.

This amounts to a catch-22 for managers from cultures with different norms for authority, communication, and collective endeavor because they must behave inauthentically in order to conform to the strictures of "authentic" leadership.

When we're in performance mode, leadership is about presenting ourselves in the most favorable light. In learning mode, we can reconcile our yearning for authenticity in how we work and lead with an equally powerful desire to grow. One leader I met was highly effective in small-group settings but struggled to convey openness to new ideas in larger meetings, where he often stuck to long-winded presentations for fear of getting derailed by others' comments. He set himself a "no PowerPoint" rule to develop a more relaxed, improvisational style. He surprised himself by how much he learned, not only about his own evolving preferences but also about the issues at hand.

Don't stick to "your story"

Most of us have personal narratives about defining moments that taught us important lessons. Consciously or not, we allow our stories, and the images of ourselves that they paint, to guide us in new situations. But the stories can become outdated as we grow, so sometimes it's necessary to alter them dramatically or even to throw them out and start from scratch.

That was true for Maria, a leader who saw herself as a "mother hen with her chicks all around." Her coach, former Ogilvy & Mather CEO Charlotte Beers, explains in *I'd Rather Be in Charge* that this self-image emerged from a time when Maria had to sacrifice her own goals and dreams to take care of her extended family. It eventually began to hold her back in her career: Though it had worked for her as a friendly and loyal team player and a peacekeeper, it wasn't helping her get the big leadership assignment she wanted. Together Maria and her coach looked for another defining moment to use as a touchstone—one that was more in keeping with Maria's desired future self, not who she had been in the past. They chose the time when Maria, as a young woman, had left her family to travel the world for 18 months. Acting from that bolder sense of self, she asked for—and got—a promotion that had previously been elusive.

Dan McAdams, a Northwestern psychology professor who has spent his career studying life stories, describes identity as "the internalized and evolving story that results from a person's selective appropriation of past, present and future." This isn't just academic jargon. McAdams is saying that you have to believe your story—but also embrace how it changes over time, according to what you need it to do. Try out new stories about yourself, and keep editing them, much as you would your résumé.

Again, revising one's story is both an introspective and a social process. The narratives we choose should not only sum up our experiences and aspirations but also reflect the demands we face and resonate with the audience we're trying to win over.

———————————

Countless books and advisers tell you to start your leadership journey with a clear sense of who you are. But that can be a recipe for staying stuck in the past. Your leadership identity can and should change each time you move on to bigger and better things.

The only way we grow as leaders is by stretching the limits of who we are—doing new things that make us uncomfortable but that teach us through direct experience who we want to become. Such growth doesn't require a radical personality makeover. Small changes—in the way we carry ourselves, the way we communicate, the way we interact—often make a world of difference in how effectively we lead.

Originally published in January–February 2015. Reprint R1501C

"Both/And" Leadership

by Wendy K. Smith, Marianne W. Lewis,
and Michael L. Tushman

JACK WELCH ONCE CLAIMED that great leaders are "relentless and boring." Management thinkers largely agree: Good leaders, so the narrative goes, are consistent in their decision making, stick to their commitments, and remain on-message. The trouble is, much as we may value consistency in our leaders, we don't live in a world that rewards it—at least not in the long term.

We all know that leaders face contradictory challenges. They may be under pressure to improve their existing products incrementally at the same time that they invent radically new products based on new business models. Or they may be striving to reach a global network while also serving distinct local needs. Some CEOs respond by prioritizing one challenge over the other; some seek an integrative middle ground, negotiating acceptable trade-offs that all stakeholders can abide by. What those approaches have in common is that they aim to provide a stable resolution of the conflicting challenges—the implicit assumption being that stability is what organizations need in order to prosper.

We disagree profoundly with this image of leadership, because it is rooted in a mischaracterization of the business environment. The challenges we focus on in this article are not conflicting goals that invite a calculated choice or a compromise. They are fundamental paradoxes that persist over time, as today's "long term" becomes tomorrow's "short term." Too much focus on one goal triggers a demand for the other. And as the business environment and the actors in it change, stability breaks down, often destroying a great deal of value and eventually culminating in a crisis that prompts a leader to impose a different order—fueling the start of another cycle.

In the following pages we propose a new model—one in which the goal of leadership is to maintain a *dynamic equilibrium* in the organization. Executives with this goal do not focus on being consistent; instead they purposefully and confidently embrace the paradoxes they confront. Senior teams build dynamic equilibrium by *separating* the imperatives that are in conflict with one another in order to recognize and respect each one (creating a separate unit to develop a new business model, for example), while at the same time actively managing *connections* between them in order to leverage interdependencies and benefit from their synergies.

The Paradoxes of Leadership

In our work with corporations over the past 20 years, we have seen that senior leaders constantly grapple with the same sets of opposing goals, which often polarize their organizations. These tensions or paradoxes fall into three categories related to three questions that many leaders perceive as "either/or" choices:

Are we managing for today or for tomorrow?

Tensions around time frame are especially salient, because a firm's long-term survival depends on experimenting, taking risks, and learning from failure in the pursuit of new products, services, and processes. However, firms also need consistency, discipline, and steady attention to make the most of the products, services, and processes they already have. These *innovation paradoxes* involve tensions between today and tomorrow, existing offerings and new ones, stability and change.

In the late 1990s, for example, senior leaders at IBM saw the internet wave cresting and realized that the company's future depended

Idea in Brief

The Problem

We look to leaders to make consistent decisions, keep a steady course, and align an organization's culture. But leaders typically face multiple demands that conflict with one another, and it's a mistake to assume there are cut-and-dried choices.

Why It Happens

Strategic paradoxes are essentially dilemmas that cannot be resolved. Tensions continually arise between today's needs and tomorrow's (innovation paradoxes), between global integration and local interests (globalization paradoxes), and between social missions and financial pressures (obligation paradoxes).

The Solution

Managers need to shift from an "either/or" mindset to a "both/and" one by seeing the virtues of inconsistency, recognizing that resources are not always finite, and embracing change rather than chasing stability. In practical terms, this means nurturing the unique aspects of competing constituencies and strategies while finding ways to unite them.

on harnessing the new technology. But IBM was also committed to sustaining its traditional strength in client-server markets. The two strategies demanded different structures, cultures, rewards, and metrics, which meant they could not be easily executed in tandem. Pursuing both involved addressing conflict between executives, as those committed to the old world and those championing the emerging world each felt their identity threatened.

Do we adhere to boundaries or cross them?

Leaders are always making and unmaking decisions around boundaries—geographic, cultural, and functional. A geographically dispersed supply chain can be wonderfully efficient, but it may lack flexibility. Dispersed innovation can produce a diversity of ideas, but certain benefits get lost when your best and brightest aren't together in one place. These *globalization paradoxes* surface tensions between global interconnection and local needs, breadth and depth, collaboration and competition.

In 2009 NASA's director of human health and performance, Jeff Davis, began pushing to generate new knowledge through collaborative cross-firm and cross-disciplinary work. Yet over the next 18 months, he faced stiff resistance from scientists protecting their turf and their identities as independent researchers. The more that technology enabled open, collaborative research, the more concerned NASA's scientists became about recognition of their individual achievements. Both collaboration and independent work were needed for the creation of new ideas, but they were organizationally and culturally incompatible.

Do we focus on creating value for our shareholders and investors or for a broader set of stakeholders?

All firms exist to create value, but leaders may be torn between maximizing profits for the firm and trying to generate wider benefits—for investors, employees, customers, and society. These tensions have mounted as public concerns about poverty and climate change have grown, as technology has helped enable and empower consumer activism, and as human capital has been increasingly recognized as the major driver of value. But being socially responsible can bring down share price, and prioritizing employees can conflict with short-term shareholders' or customers' needs. Companies struggle to address these *obligation paradoxes.*

For example, in 2010 Unilever CEO Paul Polman launched the Unilever Sustainable Living Plan, aimed at doubling the size of the business by 2020 while improving the health and well-being of more than a billion people and cutting the company's environmental impact in half. Polman argues that over the long term, social and environmental investments will lead to greater profits, whereas a singular focus on short-term profits can fuel decisions that harm our society and the environment. That is persuasive to many, but Polman faces ongoing challenges in executing the plan. Its inherent uncertainty and ambiguity have caused senior team leaders to feel a high level of anxiety and to fight about resource allocation.

These either/or questions can never be definitively answered. In part, that's because they don't really present black-and-white choices; they invite consideration of alternative demands that are interdependent as much as they are contradictory. For example, innovativeness may conflict with operational efficiency, but you can't be efficient unless you are innovative at some point—and you won't be around to be innovative unless you know how to be efficient. This interdependence is what makes the tensions strategic paradoxes, requiring leaders to reframe the questions not as classic either/or trade-offs that can be firmly resolved, but rather as ongoing "both/and" exercises ("How can we simultaneously do both X and Y?").

It is challenging, of course, to adopt a both/and approach. The relationship between the sources of a tension will change over time and in response to competitors' moves or other external events. If a company focuses on short-term performance, for instance, at the expense of innovation, the risk of not investing in innovation—and potentially missing opportunities to increase future profits—increases with time.

For Unilever, managing the competing demands of shareholders and broader stakeholders led the company to explore a more interconnected world, asking questions about how to balance global welfare and local needs. This in turn opened up debate over enhancing current products or innovating for tomorrow. Unilever's experience demonstrates that actions taken to manage any one strategic paradox will affect and maybe trigger others, which means that a piecemeal approach to managing interwoven tensions is doomed to fail.

Furthermore, the sources of a paradoxical tension are often nested in different parts or levels of an organization, which makes strategic paradoxes a major driver of internal conflict. Typically any large organization hosts many different cultures, reflecting the professional identities, networks, competencies, incentives, and geographies of the people in them. People in R&D are often scientists with identities rooted in academic disciplines and communities; they are rewarded for generating new ideas. People in marketing and sales are often close to customers, especially large customers, and they are rewarded for generating sales. In the long term, new ideas enable more sales, and more sales generate the resources to support new ideas. Yet in the short term, sales and innovation seem like competing priorities.

Practicing Paradoxical Leadership

An Interview with Terri Kelly, CEO of W.L. Gore & Associates

TERRI KELLY, WHOSE COMPANY MAKES Gore-Tex fabric and other innovative products, talked with Wendy Smith about how she manages strategic paradoxes.

Smith: What are some of the key paradoxes you have to address?
Kelly: We have a few paradoxes that we continually try to manage. One is striking the balance between meeting short-term and long-term objectives. Another one is creating the right focus on innovation and at the same time driving improvements in efficiency and effectiveness. A third one is balancing what we call the "power of our small teams" with the greater needs of the enterprise. These are all tensions we try to balance on a daily basis.

As CEO, what are you doing to manage the tensions? I try to bring them to the surface and make them explicit, so that they're right in front of people all the time—and that helps. It's important to talk about them not as a choice, where one or the other is more important, but as a balance we must continually strive to achieve. I think it's a mistake in organizations to oversimplify by conveying a sole focus on one end of the spectrum at the expense of the

Because people in each business unit tend to associate with one side or another of a paradox, real conflict can arise. CEOs and senior executives, for example, are often motivated by holding stock options, which makes them vulnerable to pressure from capital markets seeking immediate financial returns. If sales, however, are largely driven through building and maintaining long-term relationships, there is potential for a major rift: Investments that the sales force might see as necessary for goodwill could be viewed by bosses as costs ripe for cutting. Similarly, product designers at a car company might take pride in being creative engineers who build great cars, and they might resent management pressure to standardize in the pursuit of cost savings.

The inherent features of strategic paradoxes make managing in such an environment very difficult. The leader's challenge is not to choose between alternatives but to recognize that both imperatives must be addressed. Making that change from either/or to both/and thinking requires leaders to shift focus frequently in the short term in order to satisfy competing demands in the long term. Rather than

other—for example, "We must deliver short-term results." When you do this, you end up swinging guardrail to guardrail. It is much more powerful to talk about the "and" of focusing on both the short-term and the long-term objectives. By doing that, you start teaching the organization how to appreciate and deal with the inherent paradoxes.

How do you create an organization that can embed these tensions? This is the big question for us as we continue to grow. Partly we are creating different structures. For example, we realize that you need a different management structure for innovating than for managing the day-to-day business. The two activities require a different mindset, different skills, a different focus, a different time frame, and different metrics. So we establish different organizational structures to manage both, but also create clear linkages such that the teams value each other's contributions to the whole. If you separate your innovation efforts completely, you run the risk of the existing businesses rejecting what they come up with. You also miss the opportunity for the innovators to tap into key talent and resources within the existing businesses. Meanwhile, one of the expectations we have of our leaders is that they will value both activities and reinforce that within their teams.

swinging wildly between opposing forces, leaders must execute purposeful microshifts that enable growth and sustainability.

The Paradoxical Mindset

Paradoxical leadership begins with a reexamination of some implicit assumptions about leadership—which leads to movement in a new direction.

From well-intentioned consistency to consistent inconsistency

Hostility to contradictions is deeply rooted, especially in the Western world. Aristotelian logic treats contradictions and tensions as signals that we need to seek a more accurate, unified truth. If one idea is "right," its opposite must be wrong; if that seems not to be the case, then we must redefine our idea to eliminate the contradiction. We also struggle to make decisions and take actions that we see as inconsistent with an accepted truth, feeling a discomfort that psychologist Leon Festinger described as "cognitive dissonance."

The same discomfort surfaces when values conflict. A recent study at Whole Foods showed that employees understood the company's explicitly dual mission of earning profits and making the world a better place. Yet most people working in the stores identified with only one part of the mission—either the organization's profit focus or its social and environmental goals.

When two ideas seem contradictory, choosing and championing just one can minimize cognitive dissonance. It's not surprising, then, that people often deal with paradoxical tensions by picking a side and consistently supporting it. But at the top of an organization, consistency is far from a necessary virtue—indeed, it's a vice, keeping leaders from successfully dealing with strategic paradoxes. Senior executives must go into the job appreciating multiple, often conflicting, truths. They need to be consistently inconsistent and focus on managing that inconsistency. Tellingly, the Whole Foods research found that the employees most likely to move up through the leadership ranks were largely those who could effectively embrace both the financial imperatives and the social mission of the company.

From scarce resources to abundant resources

Traditional leadership approaches assume that resources—time, money, people, and so on—are limited. This is not altogether surprising when you think of the constraints that managers at lower levels of an organization face. Resources are typically fixed by a higher authority—a state of affairs that doesn't change much until *you* are the higher authority, by which time the idea that resources are limited has been baked into you. It becomes natural for executives to look for sources of constraint—and they often find them in "market expectations" or "competitor threats." But assuming that resources are constrained necessarily results in zero-sum thinking: Allocating resources to one goal means that they are no longer available for another. This fuels conflict between managers with different agendas.

In contrast, leaders who embrace paradox realize that resources, viewed in a different light, can be abundant and often generative. Rather than seeking to slice the pie thinner, people with this value-creating mindset pursue strategies to grow the pie, such as exploring collaborations with new partners, using alternative technologies, or adopting more-flexible time frames for shifting resources for better use.

Over time, committing to multiple strategies can enable more resources for each. That was the case at Zensar Technologies, an India-based provider of IT services, where leaders of the extant software franchise eventually realized that their exploratory software product could increase sales of existing products. Similarly, the coffee division of a large European food group overcame its initial resistance to an innovative proportioned-serving brewing system after seeing success in the new niche and using the new product design to increase sales of its existing brands.

From stability and certainty to dynamism and change

Leaders seek to reduce their followers' discomfort with uncertainty by asserting control—making decisions that minimize complexity and emphasize stability. This, too, is understandable: Traditional leadership and management theory was heavily influenced by studies of the military, which prizes regularity. Therefore, business managers have long been encouraged to build a common culture, where everyone is headed in the same direction, speaks the same language, and shares best practices.

But when the strategic environment changes, this approach often results in defensive and detrimental actions. As we've discussed, NASA's leaders resisted open innovation methods because scientists were invested in individual research and felt threatened by the idea of collaboration. Polaroid famously lost the battle for the digital-imaging market partly because company leaders committed to applying their successful analog-camera strategy—making money on the film, not the camera—to a market that no longer printed out pictures.

Rather than seeking stability and certainty, paradoxical leadership depends on embracing dynamism and change. Leaders must be emotionally and cognitively open to the new, developing a management strategy of coping with, rather than controlling and minimizing, ambiguity. They must be humble, even vulnerable, admitting that they might not know what the future holds. This approach emphasizes the value of experimentation and failure, spurring critical feedback to enable learning and ongoing adjustments.

For example, in the early 2000s Lego's middle managers faced tensions amid ongoing organizational change. Subordinates felt anxious and raised concerns about how their familiar practices, rules, and expectations would work in the new world. Rather than respond to these specific concerns, middle managers posed questions. They asked which parts of the current organizational approaches they should keep. They explored ways of meshing the existing world and the new one. Their questions opened up conversations that allowed both managers and subordinates to move away from seeking permanent solutions and instead develop temporary "workable certainties" that helped them move forward but were understood to be subject to future modification.

Managing Dynamic Equilibrium

When leaders assume that there are multiple truths, that resources are abundant, and that the role of management is to cope with change rather than fight it, they can help their organizations reach a state of dynamic equilibrium. This is at the center of paradoxical leadership. However, trying to shift the hearts and minds of senior team members is challenging and time-consuming. Moreover, their roles and responsibilities often lead senior people to deeply identify with one goal or another, fostering conflict. To unleash the power of paradox, therefore, leaders must build supporting organizational competencies into their senior team. This requires managers to both separate and connect opposing forces.

Separating

Tapping the potential of paradox begins with respecting the distinct needs of groups with different agendas. Doing so requires pulling apart the organization's goals and valuing each of them individually. One way to accomplish this is to create business units based on functions, geographies, or products, each with its own leader, mission, metrics, and culture. A strong sales and marketing department will focus on effectively serving its primary stakeholders (customers), while a strong finance department keeps an eye on economic efficiency and the company's image in the financial markets. Even within a function there is scope for separation into subgroups—for example, companies increasingly keep their radical-innovation teams separate from the people working on incremental improvements.

When an organization's critical tasks are intertwined, however, creating distinct units for each imperative may not be possible. Often an organization's global integration must be carried out by each of its local business units. In these situations, separation involves carving out dedicated times and spaces for exploring each goal, using different decision-making processes, or developing communication practices that enable teams to pull strategies apart.

Consider Digital Divide Data (DDD), an award-winning professional outsourcing firm that employs disadvantaged people to provide data management, research, content digitization, and other services to clients. DDD's social mission—to alleviate poverty by offering training and jobs to those in need—is intricately linked with its goal of running a sustainable business. Yet the firm's social mission and its financial demands frequently conflict, as when the leadership team considers strategic issues about whom to hire (people who are more disadvantaged or those who are more skilled) and where to expand (into regions of greater poverty or ones with more business resources). To disentangle and respect the dual missions, executives created two sets of financial statements, each with its own metrics. In board meetings CEO Jeremy Hockenstein routinely asks, "How does this decision impact our social mission?" and then, "How does this decision impact our business?"—inviting managers to consider the different needs of each strategy.

Connecting
Connecting involves finding linkages and synergies across goals. One way to do this is to build an overarching organizational identity and unite people in a higher purpose—which helps employees and executives alike to embrace the interdependence of opposing strategies. At

Two leadership approaches to competing demands

Traditional leadership differs from paradoxical leadership in its underlying assumptions about truth, resources, and management practices.

	Traditional leadership "EITHER/OR"		Paradoxical leadership "BOTH/AND"	
	Assumptions	How leaders behave	Assumptions	How leaders behave
Truth	True ideas, beliefs, and identities are internally consistent and coherent.	• Make strategic choices • Forge compromises • Keep decisions consistent with the chosen strategy • Align the firm's culture • Act consistently	True ideas, beliefs, and identities consistently embed multiple, often inconsistent, perspectives.	• Engage conflicting strategies simultaneously • Accept and value multiple cultures • Learn from multiple perspectives • Act consistently inconsistent
Resources	Resources (time, money, people, and so on) are scarce.	• Set a clear agenda • Make allocation trade-offs to best achieve priorities • Encourage competition for limited resources	Resources are abundant and can expand and generate new resources.	• Search for opportunities to grow resources, looking beyond current sources and tools • Explore new technologies and collaboration partners • Be flexible in setting time frames
Management practices	Managing involves controlling—by seeking stability and certainty.	• Adopt and apply a consistent identity across the organization • Promote best practices • Keep it simple	Managing involves coping—by embracing dynamism and change.	• Embrace multiple strategies and identities • Tolerate uncertainty • Learn from failure • Implement workable, temporary fixes and keep experimenting

NASA, Jeff Davis was able to break down his scientists' resistance to collaborative innovation when he defined his directorate's top goal this way: "We aspire to keep astronauts safe in space." In the service of safety, traditional scientists could understand the value of engaging in open-source methods. Similarly, Lego has moved beyond tensions between unabashed innovation and disciplined execution by reaffirming that it is "building the builders of tomorrow." DDD brings together its business operations and its social mission by declaring its passionate commitment to "stop the cycle of poverty."

Leaders can also design roles and processes intended to integrate separate strategic goals. For example, a leader might designate a manager to act as a business integrator, with responsibility for linking innovation with existing products. A senior manager given this assignment in a social enterprise described it as follows: "I was the bridge. I served in the role of bringing together warring camps." In other organizations, leaders use integrated metrics and reward systems to foster connections. They can also provoke conversations, asking, "How do these two goals support each other?" At DDD, Hockenstein uses this question as a key follow-up to having his top team members consider the distinctions between the firm's social mission and its financial goals.

Toward a dynamic equilibrium
Organizational success depends on both separating and connecting. In fact, doing each alone can be detrimental. Although a separate division can avoid tension in the short term, it impedes the creation of shared value in the long run, because the conflicting groups fail to benefit from one another. For example, Zensar's new software platform was initially so isolated from other units that it was unable to leverage the firm's marketing and sales capabilities. Only when the CEO encouraged his team to make structural linkages between the established products and the innovation unit was the firm able to bring its new technology to existing customers.

Connecting without separating is just as problematic. In the interest of fostering synergies, senior leaders may promote an overarching identity, stress a collective mission statement, and develop unified measurement systems. But without encouraging deep respect for the distinct value and needs of each stakeholder group, the result can be a bland compromise—a "false synergy." At worst, one point of view dominates, leaving the other to wither. Social enterprises and microfinance banks have experienced this problem. These hybrid organizations seek to address social missions through business purposes. But unless they clarify how much attention the social mission deserves, the quantifiable, focused, and short-term financial metrics often take over and drive the big decisions. Financial pressures have become so prevalent in microfinance organizations that Muhammad Yunus, founder of the Grameen Bank, has lamented that these organizations are "sacrificing microcredit for megaprofits."

To avoid these traps, smart leaders design metrics and rewards—even build out different financial statements (as at DDD)—for each strategy, and complement those with additional metrics and rewards that depend on the success of the entire organization. They create team dynamics that encourage focus on the unique needs of each strategy, while fostering respectful, trusting cultures that enable collaboration and learning. They recognize that senior team members play multiple roles—advocating for their own priorities but also considering the organization's overall needs. Most important, they demonstrate both the confidence to embrace paradoxes and the humility to know that doing so will be an ongoing challenge.

The Nobel Prize–winning physicist Niels Bohr once said, "How wonderful that we have met with a paradox. Now we have some hope of making progress." Paradox has long been at the heart of great accomplishments—revealing profound truths and spurring creativity. Advances such as Einstein's theory of relativity emerged as individuals made sense of conflicting demands. As business organizations face increasingly unpredictable, complex, and challenging environments, those that have the greatest hope of surviving and contributing to the world will have leaders who embrace strategic paradoxes.

Originally published in May 2016. Reprint R1605D

Are You a Collaborative Leader?

by Herminia Ibarra and Morten T. Hansen

WATCHING HIS EMPLOYEES use a new social technology, Marc Benioff, the CEO of Salesforce.com, had an epiphany. His company had developed Chatter, a Facebook-inspired application for companies that allows users to keep track of their colleagues and customers and share information and ideas. The employees had been trying it out internally, not just within their own work groups but across the entire organization. As Benioff read the Chatter posts, he realized that many of the people who had critical customer knowledge and were adding the most value were not even known to the management team.

The view into top management from the rank and file was just as obscure, Benioff knew. For instance, the company's annual management off-site was coming up, and he could tell from talking to employees that they wondered about what went on behind closed doors at that gathering. "They imagined we were dressing up in robes and chanting," he says.

What could he do to bring the top tier of the company closer to the workforce? Benioff asked himself. And then it hit him: Let's use Chatter to blow open the doors of the management off-site.

What greeted the 200 executives who attended that meeting was atypical. All 5,000 Salesforce.com employees had been invited to join them—virtually. Huge TV monitors placed throughout the meeting room displayed the special Chatter forum set up for the off-site. Every manager received an iPod Touch, and every table had an iPad, which attendees could use to post to the forum. A video service broadcast the meeting in real time to all employees, who could beam in and instantaneously express their views on Chatter, too.

The meeting began with the standard presentations. The managers watching them weren't quite sure what to do. Nothing unusual happened at first. Finally, Benioff grabbed the iPad on his table and made a comment on Chatter, noting what he found interesting about what was being said and adding a joke to spice it up. Some in the room followed with a few comments, and then employees watching from their offices launched a few comments back. The snowball started rolling. "Suddenly, the meeting went from a select group participating to the entire company participating," Benioff says.

Comments flew. "We felt the empowerment in the room," recalls Steve Gillmor, the head of technical media strategy.

In the end the dialogue lasted for weeks beyond the actual meeting. More important, by fostering a discussion across the entire organization, Benioff has been able to better align the whole workforce around its mission. The event served as a catalyst for the creation of a more open and empowered culture at the company.

Like Salesforce.com's managers and employees, businesspeople today are working more collaboratively than ever before, not just inside companies but also with suppliers, customers, governments, and universities. Global virtual teams are the norm, not the exception. Facebook, Twitter, LinkedIn, videoconferencing, and a host of other technologies have put connectivity on steroids and enabled new forms of collaboration that would have been impossible a short while ago.

Many executives realize that they need a new playbook for this hyperconnected environment. Those who climbed the corporate ladder in silos while using a "command and control" style can have a difficult time adjusting to the new realities. Conversely, managers who try to lead by consensus can quickly see decision making and execution grind to a halt. Crafting the right leadership style isn't easy.

Idea in Brief

A hyperconnected business world, spurred on by social media and globalization, demands a leadership style that can harness the power of connections. Leaders need to shed the command-and-control and consensus styles in favor of collaborative leadership. Our research shows that collaborative leaders who get results do four things well:

	Rather Than
Make global connections that help them spot opportunities	Focus on internal connections
Engage diverse talent from everywhere to produce results	Rely on homogeneous teams for new ideas
Collaborate at the top to model expectations	Serve corporate politics and parochial agendas
Show a strong hand to speed decisions and ensure agility	Let groups get mired in conflict or attempts at consensus

As part of our research on top-performing CEOs (see "The Best-Performing CEOs in the World," HBR, January–February 2010), we've examined what it means to be a collaborative leader. We've discovered that it requires strong skills in four areas: playing the role of connector, attracting diverse talent, modeling collaboration at the top, and showing a strong hand to keep teams from getting mired in debate. The good news is, our research also suggests that these skills can be learned—and can help executives generate exceptional long-term performance.

Play Global Connector

In his best-selling book *The Tipping Point,* Malcolm Gladwell used the term "connector" to describe individuals who have many ties to different social worlds. It's not the number of people they know that makes connectors significant, however; it's their ability to link people, ideas, and resources that wouldn't normally bump into

Play Global Connector

- Do you attend conferences outside your professional specialty?

- Are you part of a global network like Young Presidents' Organization?

- Do you regularly blog or e-mail employees about trends, ideas, and people you encounter outside your organization?

- How often do you meet with parties outside your company (competitors, consumers, government officials, university contacts, and so on) who are not directly relevant to your immediate job demands or current operations?

- Are you on the board of any outside organizations?

---

one another. In business, connectors are critical facilitators of collaboration.

For David Kenny, the president of Akamai Technologies, being a connector is one of the most important ways he adds value. He spends much of his time traveling around the world to meet with employees, partners, and customers. "I spend time with media owners to hear what they think about digital platforms, Facebook, and new pricing models, and with Microsoft leaders to get their views on cloud computing," he says. "I'm interested in hearing how our clients feel about macroeconomic issues, the G20, and how debt will affect future generations." These conversations lead to new strategic insights and relationships, and help Akamai develop critical external partnerships.

Connecting the world outside to people inside the company is crucial to Kenny. He uses a number of tactics to do this. "First, I check in on Foursquare often and post my location to Facebook and Twitter," he says. "It lets employees in different Akamai locations know I'm in town so that anybody at any level can bring me suggestions or concerns. Second, every time I go to one of our locations, I have lunch or coffee with 20 to 40 people. We go around the room, and people ask questions on topics they most want to address. Often my answer is to connect them with others in Akamai or even people at other companies who have expertise on the topic. Third, if I see a big opportunity when meeting with a customer or colleague, I will schedule a follow-up visit and bring along the right experts from Akamai. Fourth, whenever I travel, I try to make room to meet with two to three people I know in that location. Whenever possible, I bring someone else from Akamai with me to those meetings."

Kenny's networking recently resulted in an important strategic alliance with Ericsson. Akamai is now working with the mobile giant to change consumers' internet experiences on mobile devices. The partnership evolved out of a conversation Kenny had with a mid-level Ericsson executive two years ago at the Monaco Media Forum. "It really changed my idea of what Ericsson could be, and I saw that we were both trying to solve a similar technical problem," Kenny says. "Then I worked through mutual friends to meet their CEO and arranged for the right people on his team to meet with their Akamai counterparts."

Presidents and CEOs aren't the only executives building bridges between their organizations and the outside world nowadays. Take Beth Comstock, the chief marketing officer of General Electric. She is famous for her weekly "BlackBerry Beth" blog, in which she shares what she has learned in her external role for busy (and perhaps more internally focused) GE managers. The pithy and provocative blog goes out to thousands of GE's sales, marketing, and technology leaders. In it, Comstock passes along interesting information that people might have missed, taking care to tie it back to challenges and opportunities GE faces. For example, in a recent post from the World Economic Forum, she reported that a panel of scientists had come to the same conclusion that a GE survey had—that technology alone cannot ensure innovation and that more training in creativity is needed.

"I work hard to curate information that I don't believe many at GE will have heard and to translate information in a way that is relevant to our challenges," says Comstock. "I probably spend half of my time immersed in worlds beyond GE. I hope this encourages my colleagues to be more externally focused. The message is 'If I find it important to spend some of my time this way, maybe you will, too.'"

To connect their organizations to the wider world, collaborative leaders develop contacts not only in the typical areas—local clubs, industry associations, and customer and supplier relations—but beyond them. Networking in adjacent industries, innovation hot spots like Silicon Valley, or emerging economies or with people of different educational or ethnic backgrounds helps open their eyes to new business opportunities and partners. For example, Comstock's external contacts in the innovation space led GE to NASA, with which the corporation has shared insights and best practices. The two organizations have also begun discussions about space technologies that might have applications in health care.

Engage Talent at the Periphery

Research has consistently shown that diverse teams produce better results, provided they are well led. The ability to bring together people from different backgrounds, disciplines, cultures, and generations and leverage all they have to offer, therefore, is a must-have for leaders. Yet many companies spend inordinate amounts of time, money, and energy attracting talented employees only to subject them to homogenizing processes that kill creativity. In a lot of multinational companies, for example, nonnative English speakers are at a disadvantage. To senior management, they don't sound as "leaderlike" as the Anglophones, and they end up getting passed over for promotions. At a time when innovations are increasingly originating in emerging markets, companies that allow this to happen lose out.

France's Danone, one of the top performers in our research, makes sure its executives don't encounter such obstacles. When all the managers worldwide get together for the company's annual strategic review, many choose to present in their native tongue. Says CEO Franck Riboud: "We spend a fortune on interpreters so that being less articulate in English is not a barrier. Some of our executives have even presented their business case in native dress. This helps us steal away talent from competitors where those who don't speak perfect English get stuck."

Reckitt Benckiser, the UK-based producer of home, health, and personal care products and another top performer in our research, considers the diversity of its workforce to be one of its competitive advantages—and a key reason it has seen net income grow 17%

Engage Talent at the Periphery

- How diverse is your immediate team in terms of nationality? Gender? Age?
- How much time do you spend outside your home country?
- Have you visited your emerging markets this year?
- Does your network include people in their twenties (who *aren't* your kids)?

annually, on average, from 1999 to 2010. No nationality dominates the company's senior team. Two executives are Dutch, one is German, two are British, one is South African, two are Italian, and one is from India. According to (soon-to-retire) CEO Bart Becht: "It doesn't matter whether I have a Pakistani, a Chinese person, a Brit, or a Turk, man or woman, sitting in the same room, or whether I have people from sales or something else, so long as I have people with different experiences—because the chance for new ideas is much greater when you have people with different backgrounds. The chance for conflict is also higher—and conflict is good per se, as long as it's constructive and gets us to the best idea."

As Becht suggests, nationality isn't the only kind of diversity that matters. Research on creative industries shows that the collaborations that are most successful (whether in terms of patent citation, critical acclaim, or financial return) include both experienced people and newcomers and bring together people who haven't worked with one another before. Leaders need to make a concerted effort to promote this mix: Left to their own devices, people will choose to collaborate with others they know well or who have similar backgrounds. Static groups breed insularity, which can be deadly for innovation. Nokia's former executive team, for example, was 100% Finnish and had worked closely together for more than a decade. Many believe homogeneity explains why the team failed to see the smartphone threat emerging from Silicon Valley.

Collaborative leaders ensure that teams stay fresh via periodic infusions of new players. Including employees from Generation Y—those born from the mid-1970s to the early 2000s, who have grown up sharing knowledge and opinions online—is another obvious way to enliven collaborations. A number of leading companies have begun using technology to harness Gen Y ideas and perspectives. Salesforce.com, as we have seen, brought them in from the periphery by using Chatter to open its management off-site to all staff. At India's HCL, employees throughout the company join virtual conversations on topics that are important to them, and CEO Vineet Nayar reaches out personally through a popular blog that allows him to interact with a broad cross section of employees. In a market where the competition for engineering talent is fierce, the ability to attract the best and brightest helped HCL grow 30% annually from 2008 to 2010.

Collaborate at the Top First

It's not enough for leaders to spot collaborative opportunities and attract the best talent to them. They must also set the tone by being good collaborators themselves. All too often, efforts to collaborate in the middle are sabotaged by political games and turf battles higher up in the organization. Consider that Microsoft, according to a former company executive writing in the *New York Times* last year, developed a viable tablet computer more than a decade ago but failed to preempt Apple's smash hit because competing Microsoft divisions conspired to kill the project.

Part of the problem is that many leadership teams, composed of the CEO and his or her direct reports, actually don't operate as teams. Each member runs his or her own region, function, or product or service category, without much responsibility—or incentive— for aligning the organization's various projects and operations into a coherent whole.

At Brazil's Natura Cosméticos, CEO Alessandro Carlucci has instituted a comprehensive "engagement process" that promotes a collaborative mindset at all levels and has helped the firm win a top spot on *Fortune*'s list of best companies for leaders. The process was implemented after Natura's highly successful IPO in 2004, when

Collaborate at the Top First

- Do members of your team have any joint responsibilities beyond their individual goals?

- Does the compensation of your direct reports depend on any collective goals or reflect any collective responsibilities?

- What specifically have you done to eradicate power struggles within your team?

- Do your direct reports have both performance and learning goals?

competing agendas among the senior managers began to threaten the company's prospects. Carlucci decided he needed to reorganize the executive committee to unify its members around common goals and stop the power struggles. He asked the members of the top team to make a commitment to self-development as part of their stewardship of the company.

Each executive embarked on a "personal journey" with an external coach, who met with everyone individually and with the team as a group. "It is a different type of coaching," Carlucci explains. "It's not just talking to your boss or subordinates but talking about a person's life history, with their families; it is more holistic, broader, integrating all the different roles of a human being."

Roberto Pedote, Natura's senior vice president for finance, IT, and legal affairs, adds: "I think that the main point is that we are making ourselves vulnerable, showing that we are not supermen, that we have failures; that we are afraid of some things and we don't have all the answers."

Since the engagement process was adopted, Natura's executives have become much better at teaming up on efforts to improve the business, which grew by 21% in 2010. The collaborative mindset at the top has cascaded down to the rest of the organization, and the process has been rolled out to all the company's managers.

If leaders are to encourage more innovation through partnerships across sectors and with suppliers, customers, and consumers, they need to stop relying heavily on short-term performance

Collaboration Does Not Equal Consensus

COLLABORATIVE LEADERSHIP IS THE CAPACITY to engage people and groups outside one's formal control and inspire them to work toward common goals—despite differences in convictions, cultural values, and operating norms.

Most people understand intuitively that collaborative leadership is the opposite of the old command-and-control model, but the differences with a consensus-based approach are more nuanced. Below are some helpful distinctions between the three leadership styles.

Comparing three styles of leadership

	Command and control	Consensus	Collaborative
Organizational structure	Hierarchy	Matrix or small group	Dispersed, cross-organizational network
Who has the relevant information?	Senior management	Formally designated members or representatives of the relevant geographies and disciplines	Employees at all levels and locations and a variety of external stakeholders
Who has the authority to make final decisions?	The people at the top of the organization have clear authority	All parties have equal authority	The people leading collaborations have clear authority
What is the basis for accountability and control?	Financial results against plan	Many performance indicators, by function or geography	Performance on achieving shared goals
Where does it work best?	Works well within a defined hierarchy; works poorly for complex organizations and when innovation is important	Works in small teams; works poorly when speed is important	Works well for diverse groups and cross-unit and cross-company work, and when innovation and creativity are critical

indicators. According to the psychologist Carol Dweck, people are driven to do tasks by either performance or learning goals. When performance goals dominate an environment, people are motivated to show others that they have a valued attribute, such as intelligence or leadership. When learning goals dominate, they are motivated to *develop* the attribute. Performance goals, she finds, induce people to favor tasks that will make them look good over tasks that will help them learn. A shift toward learning goals will make managers more open to exploring opportunities to acquire knowledge from others.

At HCL, CEO Vineet Nayar demonstrated his commitment to collaboration by adopting a radically different 360-degree evaluation for his top managers—one that invited a wide range of employees to weigh in. Although the company had done 360-degree reviews before, each manager had been assessed by a relatively small number of people, mostly within the manager's immediate span of control. As Nayar recalls in his book *Employees First, Customers Second* (Harvard Business Review Press, 2010), "most of the respondents operated within the same area as the person they were evaluating. This reinforced the boundaries between the parts of the pyramid. But we were trying to change all that. We wanted to encourage people to operate across these boundaries." Nayar set the tone by posting his own 360-degree evaluation on the web. Once executives got used to the new transparency, the 360-degree reviews were expanded to a broader group. A new feature, "Happy Feet," was added, allowing all employees whom a manager might affect or influence to evaluate that manager—regardless of their reporting relationship.

Depoliticizing senior management so that executives are rewarded for collaborating rather than promoting their individual agendas is an absolute essential. At Reckitt Benckiser, there's little tolerance for politics. Says Bart Becht: "We go out of our way to make sure that politics get eradicated, because I think they're very bad for an organization. I think they're poison, to be honest with you." Becht's direct, no-nonsense style and the expectation that people should openly disagree with one another in meetings also help keep politics to a minimum, allowing real teamwork to take hold.

Show a Strong Hand

Once leaders start getting employees to collaborate, they face a different problem: overdoing it. Too often people will try to collaborate on everything and wind up in endless meetings, debating ideas and struggling to find consensus. They can't reach decisions and execute quickly. Collaboration becomes not the oil greasing the wheel but the sand grinding it to a halt.

Effective collaborative leaders assume a strong role directing teams. They maintain agility by forming and disbanding them as opportunities come and go—in much the same way that Hollywood producers, directors, actors, writers, and technicians establish teams for the life of movie projects. Collaborative efforts are highly fluid and not confined to company silos.

Effective leaders also assign clear decision rights and responsibilities, so that at the appropriate point someone can end the discussion and make a final call. Although constructive confrontation and tempered disagreements are encouraged, battles aren't left raging on. This is exactly how things work at Reckitt Benckiser. When teams meet, people know that it is OK—in fact expected—to propose ideas and challenge one another. They debate loudly and furiously until the best idea wins. If no obvious agreement is reached in time, the person chairing the meeting normally makes a decision and the rest of the group falls in line. This ensures vigorous debate but clear decisions and quick action—diversity in counsel, unity in command, as Cyrus the Great once said.

Loosening Control Without Losing Control

In the old world of silos and solo players, leaders had access to everything they needed under one roof, and a command-and-control style served them well. But things have changed: The world has become much more interconnected, and if executives don't know how to tap into the power of those connections, they'll be left behind.

Leaders today must be able to harness ideas, people, and resources from across boundaries of all kinds. That requires reinventing their

Show a Strong Hand

- Have you killed any collaboration projects in the past six months?

- Do you manage dynamically—forming and disbanding teams quickly as opportunities arise?

- Do the right people in your organization know they can "close" a discussion and make a decision?

- Does your team debate ideas vigorously but then unite behind decisions made?

talent strategies and building strong connections both inside and outside their organizations. To get all the disparate players to work together effectively, they also need to know when to wield influence rather than authority to move things forward, and when to halt unproductive discussions, squash politicking, and make final calls.

Differences in convictions, cultural values, and operating norms inevitably add complexity to collaborative efforts. But they also make them richer, more innovative, and more valuable. Getting that value is the heart of collaborative leadership.

Originally published in July–August 2011. Reprint R1107D

Cross-Silo Leadership

*by Tiziana Casciaro, Amy C. Edmondson,
and Sujin Jang*

THOUGH MOST EXECUTIVES recognize the importance of breaking down silos to help people collaborate across boundaries, they struggle to make it happen. That's understandable: It is devilishly difficult.

Think about your own relationships at work—the people you report to and those who report to you, for starters. Now consider the people in other functions, units, or geographies whose work touches yours in some way. Which relationships get prioritized in your day-to-day job?

We've posed that question to managers, engineers, salespeople, and consultants in companies around the world. The response we get is almost always the same: vertical relationships.

But when we ask, "Which relationships are most important for creating value for customers?" the answers flip. Today the vast majority of innovation and business-development opportunities lie in the interfaces between functions, offices, or organizations. In short, the integrated solutions that most customers want—but companies wrestle with developing—require horizontal collaboration.

The value of horizontal teamwork is widely recognized. Employees who can reach outside their silos to find colleagues with complementary expertise learn more, sell more, and gain skills faster. Harvard's Heidi Gardner has found that firms with more cross-boundary collaboration achieve greater customer loyalty and higher margins. As innovation hinges more and more on interdisciplinary cooperation, digitalization transforms business at a breakneck pace, and globalization increasingly requires people to work across national borders, the demand for executives who can lead projects at interfaces keeps rising.

Our research and consulting work with hundreds of executives and managers in dozens of organizations confirms both the need for and the challenge of horizontal collaboration. "There's no doubt. We should focus on big projects that call for integration across practices," a partner in a global accounting firm told us. "That's where our greatest distinctive value is developed. But most of us confine ourselves to the smaller projects that we can handle within our practice areas. It's frustrating." A senior partner in a leading consulting firm put it slightly differently: "You know you should swim farther to catch a bigger fish, but it is a lot easier to swim in your own pond and catch a bunch of small fish."

One way to break down silos is to redesign the formal organizational structure. But that approach has limits: It's costly, confusing, and slow. Worse, every new structure solves some problems but creates others. That's why we've focused on identifying activities that facilitate boundary crossing. We've found that people can be trained to see and connect with pools of expertise throughout their organizations and to work better with colleagues who think very differently from them. The core challenges of operating effectively at interfaces are simple: *learning* about people on the other side and *relating* to them. But simple does not mean easy; human beings have always struggled to understand and relate to those who are different.

Leaders need to help people develop the capacity to overcome these challenges on both individual and organizational levels. That means providing training in and support for four practices that enable effective interface work.

1. Develop and Deploy Cultural Brokers

Fortunately, in most companies there are people who already excel at interface collaboration. They usually have experiences and relationships that span multiple sectors, functions, or domains

Idea in Brief

The Challenge

Innovation initiatives, globalization, and digitalization increasingly require people to collaborate across functional and national boundaries. But breaking down silos remains frustratingly difficult.

The Cause

Employees don't know how to identify expertise outside their own work domains and struggle to understand the perspectives of colleagues who think very differently from them.

The Solution

Leaders can help employees connect with and relate to people across organizational divides by doing four things: developing and deploying "cultural brokers," who help groups overcome differences; encouraging and training workers to ask the right questions; getting people to see things through others' eyes; and broadening everyone's vision of networks of expertise inside and outside the company.

and informally serve as links between them. We call these people *cultural brokers*. In studies involving more than 2,000 global teams, one of us—Sujin—found that diverse teams containing a cultural broker significantly outperformed diverse teams without one. (See "The Most Creative Teams Have a Specific Type of Cultural Diversity," HBR.org, July 24, 2018.) Companies should identify these individuals and help them increase their impact.

Cultural brokers promote cross-boundary work in one of two ways: by acting as a *bridge* or as an *adhesive*.

A bridge offers himself as a go-between, allowing people in different functions or geographies to collaborate with minimal disruption to their day-to-day routine. Bridges are most effective when they have considerable knowledge of both sides and can figure out what each one needs. This is why the champagne and spirits distributor Moët Hennessy España hired two enologists, or wine experts, to help coordinate the work of its marketing and sales groups, which had a history of miscommunication and conflict. The enologists could relate to both groups equally: They could speak to marketers about the emotional content (the ephemeral "bouquet") of brands, while also providing pragmatic salespeople with details on the distinctive features of products they needed to win over retailers. Understanding both worlds, the enologists were able to communicate the rationale for each group's modus operandi to the other, allowing marketing and sales to work more synergistically even without directly interacting. This kind of cultural brokerage is efficient because it lets disparate parties work around differences without investing in learning the other side's perspective or changing how they work. It's especially valuable for one-off collaborations or when the company is under intense time pressure to deliver results.

Adhesives, in contrast, bring people together and help build mutual understanding and lasting relationships. Take one manager we spoke with at National Instruments, a global producer of automated test equipment. He frequently connects colleagues from different regions and functions. "I think of it as building up the relationships between them," he told us. "If a colleague needs to work with someone in another office or function, I would tell them, 'OK, here's the person to call.' Then I'd take the time to sit down and say, 'Well, let me tell you a little bit about how these guys work.'" Adhesives facilitate collaboration by vouching for people and helping them decipher one another's language. Unlike bridges, adhesives develop others' capacity to work across a boundary in the future without their assistance.

Company leaders can build both bridging and adhesive capabilities in their organizations by hiring people with multifunctional or multicultural backgrounds who have the strong interpersonal skills needed to build rapport with multiple parties. Because it takes resilience to work with people across cultural divides, firms should also look for a *growth mindset*—the desire to learn and to take on challenges and "stretch" opportunities.

In addition, leaders can develop more brokers by giving people at all levels the chance to move into roles that expose them to multiple parts of the company. This, by the way, is good training for general managers and is what many rotational leadership-development programs aim to accomplish. Claudine Wolfe, the head of talent and development at the global insurer Chubb, maintains that the company's capacity to serve customers around the world rests on giving top performers opportunities to work in different geographies and cultivate an international mindset. "We give people their critical development experiences steeped in the job, in the region," she says. "They get coaching in the cultural norms and the language, but then they live it and internalize it. They go to the local bodega, take notice of the products on the shelves, have conversations with the merchant, and learn what it really means to live in that environment."

Matrix organizational structures, in which people report to two (or more) groups, can also help develop cultural brokers. Despite their inherent challenges (they can be infuriatingly hard to navigate without strong leadership and accountability), matrices get people used to operating at interfaces.

We're not saying that everyone in your organization needs to be a full-fledged cultural broker. But consciously expanding the ranks of brokers and deploying them to grease the wheels of collaboration can go a long way.

2. Encourage People to Ask the Right Questions

It's nearly impossible to work across boundaries without asking a lot of questions. Inquiry is critical because what we see and take for granted on one side of an interface is not the same as what people experience on the other side.

Indeed, a study of more than 1,000 middle managers at a large bank that Tiziana conducted with Bill McEvily and Evelyn Zhang of the University of Toronto and Francesca Gino of Harvard Business School highlights the value of inquisitiveness in boundary-crossing work. It showed that managers with high levels of curiosity were more likely to build networks that spanned disconnected parts of the company.

But all of us are vulnerable to forgetting the crucial practice of asking questions as we move up the ladder. High-achieving people in particular frequently fail to wonder what others are seeing. Worse, when we do recognize that we don't know something, we may avoid asking a question out of (misguided) fear that it will make us look incompetent or weak. "Not asking questions is a big mistake many professionals make," Norma Kraay, the managing partner of talent for Deloitte Canada, told us. "Expert advisers want to offer a solution. That's what they're trained to do."

Leaders can encourage inquiry in two important ways—and in the process help create an organization where it's psychologically safe to ask questions.

Be a role model

When leaders show interest in what others are seeing and thinking by asking questions, it has a stunning effect: It prompts people in their organizations to do the same.

Asking questions also conveys the humility that more and more business leaders and researchers are pointing to as vital to success. According to Laszlo Bock, Google's former senior vice president of people operations, humble people are better at bringing others together to solve tough problems. In a fast-changing business environment, humility—not to be confused with false modesty—is simply a strength. Its power comes from realism (as in *It really is a complex, challenging world out there; if we don't work together, we don't stand a chance*).

Gino says one way a leader can make employees feel comfortable asking questions is by openly acknowledging when he or she doesn't know the answer. Another, she says, is by having days in which employees are explicitly encouraged to ask "Why?" "What if . . . ?" and "How might we . . . ?" (See "The Business Case for Curiosity," HBR, September–October 2018.)

Teach employees the art of inquiry

Training can help expand the range and frequency of questions employees ask and, according to Hal Gregersen of the MIT Leadership Center, can reinvigorate their sense of curiosity. But some questions are better than others. (See the exhibit "How to ask good questions.") And if you simply tell people to raise more questions, you might unleash interrogation tactics that inhibit rather than encourage the development of new perspectives. As MIT's Edgar

How to ask good questions

Common pitfalls	Effective inquiry
Start with yes-or-no questions.	Start with open-ended questions that minimize preconceptions. ("How are things going on your end?" "What does your group see as the key opportunity in this space?")
Continue asking overly general questions ("What's on your mind?") that may invite long off-point responses.	As collaborations develop, ask questions that focus on specific issues but allow people plenty of room to elaborate. ("What do you know about x?" "Can you explain how that works?")
Assume that you've grasped what speakers intended.	Check your understanding by summarizing what you're hearing and asking explicitly for corrections or missing elements. ("Does that sound right—am I missing anything?" "Can you help me fill in the gaps?")
Assume the collaboration process will take care of itself.	Periodically take time to inquire into others' experiences of the process or relationship. ("How do you think the project is going?" "What could we do to work together more effectively?")

Schein explains in his book *Humble Inquiry,* questions are the secret to productive work relationships—but they must be driven by genuine interest in understanding another's view.

It's also important to learn how to request information in the least biased way possible. This means asking open-ended questions that minimize preconceptions, rather than yes-or-no questions. For instance, "What do you see as the key opportunity in this space?" will generate a richer dialogue than "Do you think this is the right opportunity to pursue?"

As collaborations move forward, it's helpful for team leaders or project managers to raise queries that encourage others to dive more deeply into specific issues and express related ideas or experiences. "What do you know about *x?*" and "Can you explain how that works?" are two examples. These questions are focused but neither limit responses nor invite long discourses that stray too far from the issue at hand.

How you process the answers also matters. It's natural, as conversations unfold, to assume you understand what's being said. But what people hear is biased by their expertise and experiences. So it's important to train people to check whether they're truly getting their colleagues' meaning, by using language like "This is what I'm hearing—did I miss anything?" or "Can you help me fill in the gaps?" or "I think what you said means the project is on track. Is that correct?"

Finally, periodic temperature taking is needed to examine the collaborative process itself. The only way to find out how others are experiencing a project or relationship is by asking questions such as "How do you think the project is going?" and "What could we do to work together more effectively?"

3. Get People to See the World Through Others' Eyes

Leaders shouldn't just encourage employees to be curious about different groups and ask questions about their thinking and practices; they should also urge their people to actively consider others' points of view. People from different organizational groups don't see things the same way. Studies (including research on barriers to successful product innovation that the management professor Deborah Dougherty conducted at Wharton) consistently reveal that this leads to misunderstandings in interface work. It's vital, therefore, to help people learn how to take the perspectives of others. One of us, Amy, has done research showing that ambitious cross-industry innovation projects succeed when diverse participants discover how to do this. New Songdo, a project to build a city from scratch in South Korea that launched a decade ago, provides an instructive example. Early in the effort, project leaders brought together architects, engineers, planners, and environmental experts and helped them integrate their expertise in a carefully crafted learning process designed to break down barriers between disciplines. Today, in striking contrast to other "smart" city projects, New Songdo is 50% complete and has 30,000 residents, 33,000 jobs, and emissions that are 70% lower than those of other developments its size.

In a study of jazz bands and Broadway productions, Brian Uzzi of Northwestern University found that leaders of successful teams had an unusual ability to assume other people's viewpoints. These leaders could speak the multiple "languages" of their teammates. Other research has shown that when members of a diverse team proactively take the perspectives of others, it enhances the positive effect of information sharing and increases the team's creativity.

Creating a culture that fosters this kind of behavior is a senior leadership responsibility. Psychological research suggests that while most people are *capable* of taking others' perspectives, they are rarely *motivated* to do so. Leaders can provide some motivation by emphasizing to their teams how much the integration of diverse expertise enhances new value creation. But a couple of other tactics will help:

Organize cross-silo dialogues

Instead of holding one-way information sessions, leaders should set up cross-silo discussions that help employees see the world through the eyes of customers or colleagues in other parts of the company. The goal is to get everyone to share knowledge and work on synthesizing that diverse input into new solutions. This happens best in face-to-face meetings that are carefully structured to allow people time to listen to one another's thinking. Sometimes the process includes customers; one consulting firm we know started to replace traditional meetings, at which the firm conveyed information to clients, with a workshop format designed to explore questions and develop solutions in *collaboration* with them. The new format gives both the clients and the consultants a chance to learn from each other.

One of the more thoughtful uses of cross-silo dialogue is the "focused event analysis" (FEA) at Children's Minnesota. In an FEA people from the health system's different clinical and operational groups come together after a failure, such as the administration of the wrong medication to a patient. One at a time participants offer their take on what happened; the goal is to carefully document multiple perspectives *before* trying to identify a cause. Often participants are surprised to learn how people from other groups saw the incident. The assumption underlying the FEA is that most failures have not one root cause but many. Once the folks involved have a multifunctional picture of the contributing factors, they can alter procedures and systems to prevent similar failures.

Hire for curiosity and empathy
You can boost your company's capacity to see the world from different perspectives by bringing on board people who relate to and sympathize with the feelings, thoughts, and attitudes of others. Southwest Airlines, which hires fewer than 2% of all applicants, selects people with empathy and enthusiasm for customer service, evaluating them through behavioral interviews ("Tell me about a time when . . .") and team interviews in which candidates are observed interacting.

4. Broaden Your Employees' Vision

You can't lead at the interfaces if you don't know where they are. Yet many organizations unwittingly encourage employees to never look beyond their own immediate environment, such as their function or business unit, and as a result miss out on potential insights employees could get if they scanned more-distant networks. Here are some ways that leaders can create opportunities for employees to widen their horizons, both within the company and beyond it:

Bring employees from diverse groups together on initiatives
As a rule, cross-functional teams give people across silos a chance to identify various kinds of expertise within their organization, map how they're connected or disconnected, and see how the internal knowledge network can be linked to enable valuable collaboration.

At one global consulting firm, the leader of the digital health-care practice used to have its consultants speak just to clients' CIOs and CTOs. But she realized that that "unnecessarily limited the practice's ability to identify opportunities to serve clients beyond IT," she says. So she began to set up sessions with the entire C-suite at clients and brought in consultants from across all her firm's health-care practices—including systems redesign, operations excellence, strategy, and financing—to provide a more integrated look at the firm's health-care innovation expertise.

Those meetings allowed the consultants to discover the connections among the practices in the health-care division, identify the people best positioned to bridge the different practices, and see novel ways to combine the firm's various kinds of expertise to meet clients' needs. That helped the consultants spot value-generating opportunities for services at the interfaces between the practices. The new approach was so effective that, in short order, the leader was asked to head up a new practice that served as an interface across all the practices in the IT division so that she could replicate her success in other parts of the firm.

Urge employees to explore distant networks

Employees also need to be pushed to tap into expertise outside the company and even outside the industry. The domains of human knowledge span science, technology, business, geography, politics, history, the arts, the humanities, and beyond, and any interface between them could hold new business opportunities. Consider the work of the innovation consultancy IDEO. By bringing design techniques from technology, science, and the arts to business, it has been able to create revolutionary products, like the first Apple mouse (which it developed from a Xerox PARC prototype into a commercial offering), and help companies in many industries embrace design thinking as an innovation strategy.

The tricky part is finding the domains most relevant to key business goals. Although many innovations have stemmed from what Abraham Flexner, the founding director of the Institute for

Advanced Study, called "the usefulness of useless knowledge," businesses can ill afford to rely on open-ended exploratory search alone. To avoid this fate, leaders can take one of two approaches:

A *top-down approach* works when the knowledge domains with high potential for value creation have already been identified. For example, a partner in an accounting firm who sees machine learning as key to the profession's future might have an interested consultant or analyst in her practice take online courses or attend industry conferences about the technology and ask that person to come back with ideas about its implications. The partner might organize workshops in which the junior employee shares takeaways from the learning experiences and brainstorms, with experienced colleagues, potential applications in the firm.

A *bottom-up approach* is better when leaders have trouble determining which outside domains the organization should connect with—a growing challenge given the speed at which new knowledge is being created. Increasingly, leaders must rely on employees to identify and forge connections with far-flung domains. One approach is to crowdsource ideas for promising interfaces—for example, by inviting employees to propose conferences in other industries they'd like to attend, courses on new skill sets they'd like to take, or domain experts they'd like to bring in for workshops. It's also critical to give employees the time and resources to scan external domains and build connections to them.

Breaking Down Silos

In today's economy everyone knows that finding new ways to combine an organization's diverse knowledge is a winning strategy for creating lasting value. But it doesn't happen unless employees have the opportunities and tools to work together productively across silos. To unleash the potential of horizontal collaboration, leaders must equip people to learn and to relate to one another across cultural and logistical divides. The four practices we've just described can help.

Not only is each one useful on its own in tackling the distinct challenges of interface work, but together these practices are mutually enhancing: Engaging in one promotes competency in another. Deploying cultural brokers who build connections across groups gets people to ask questions and learn what employees in other groups are thinking. When people start asking better questions, they're immediately better positioned to understand others' perspectives and challenges. Seeing things from someone else's perspective— walking in his or her moccasins—in turn makes it easier to detect more pockets of knowledge. And network scanning illuminates interfaces where cultural brokers might be able to help groups collaborate effectively.

Over time these practices—none of which require advanced degrees or deep technical smarts—dissolve the barriers that make boundary-crossing work so difficult. When leaders create conditions that encourage and support these practices, collaboration across the interface will ultimately become second nature.

Originally published in May–June 2019. Reprint R1903J

How CEOs Manage Time

by Michael E. Porter and Nitin Nohria

IN THE LEXICON OF MANAGEMENT, the CEO is the epitome of leadership. Yet surprisingly little is known about this unique role. While CEOs are the ultimate power in their companies, they face challenges and constraints that few others recognize.

Running a large global company is an exceedingly complex job. The scope of the organization's managerial work is vast, encompassing functional agendas, business unit agendas, multiple organizational levels, and myriad external issues. It also involves a wide array of constituencies—shareholders, customers, employees, the board, the media, government, community organizations, and more. Unlike any other executive, the CEO has to engage with them all. On top of that, the CEO must be the internal and external face of the organization through good times and bad.

CEOs, of course, have a great deal of help and resources at their disposal. However, they, more than anyone else in the organization, confront an acute scarcity of one resource. That resource is *time*. There is never enough time to do everything that a CEO is responsible for. Despite this, CEOs remain accountable for *all* the work of their organizations.

The way CEOs allocate their time and their presence—where they choose to personally participate—is crucial, not only to their own effectiveness but also to the performance of their companies. Where and how CEOs are involved determines what gets done and signals priorities for others. It also affects their legitimacy. A CEO who doesn't spend enough time with colleagues will seem insular and out of touch, whereas one who spends too much time in direct decision making will risk being seen as a micromanager and erode employees' initiative. A CEO's schedule (indeed, any leader's schedule), then, is a manifestation of *how* the leader leads and sends powerful messages to the rest of the organization.

A crucial missing link in understanding the time allocation of CEOs—and making it more effective—has been systematic data on what they actually do. Research on that has tended either to cover a small handful of CEOs, like the 1973 study in which Henry Mintzberg closely observed five chief executives (some of whom led nonprofits) for five days each, or to rely on large surveys that cover short periods (such as our HBS colleague Raffaella Sadun's 2017 study based on daily phone surveys with 1,114 CEOs from a wide variety of companies in six countries over one week).

Our study, which we launched in 2006, offers the first comprehensive and detailed examination of CEO time use in large, complex companies over an extended period. To date, we have tracked the time allocation of 27 CEOs—two women and 25 men—for a full quarter (three months) each. Their companies, which are primarily public, had an average annual revenue of $13.1 billion during the study period. These leaders were all participants in the New CEO Workshop, an intensive program that every year brings newly appointed CEOs of large companies to Harvard Business School in two cohorts of 10 to 12 each. In total just over 300 CEOs have attended it.

In the study each CEO's executive assistant (EA) was trained to code the CEO's time in 15-minute increments, 24 hours a day and seven days a week, and to regularly verify that coding with the CEO. The resulting data set reveals where, how, and with whom the CEO spent his or her time and on what activities, topics, and tasks. Because it also covers what CEOs do outside of work, we have visibility into how CEOs balance work and personal life. In all, we collected and coded data on nearly 60,000 CEO hours.

After CEOs completed the time-tracking phase, we shared their data with them, comparing it with anonymized data of the other

Idea in Brief

The Problem

Managing the immense demands on their time is one of the biggest challenges CEOs face. Yet knowledge about how CEOs actually use time is almost nonexistent.

The Study

The authors tracked the activities of CEOs at 27 large companies 24/7 for 13 weeks and then held intensive debriefs with them. The resulting data set offers deep insights not just into time management but into the CEO's role itself.

The Findings

Leaders must learn to simultaneously manage seemingly contradictory dualities—integrating direct decision making with indirect levers like strategy and culture, balancing internal and external constituencies, proactively driving an agenda while responding to unfolding events, exercising leverage while being mindful of constraints, focusing on tangible decisions and the symbolic significance of every action, and combining formal power and legitimacy.

CEOs we had studied up to that point. These intensive debriefings often included the CEOs' reflections on the pressures they faced in managing time, and on their mistakes and lessons learned. We also shared our accumulated data with the participants in each New CEO Workshop. In our discussions, CEOs routinely described managing time as one of their greatest challenges. The observations, questions, and personal approaches to allocating time they shared further enriched our understanding.

In this article we will do three things:

First, we'll provide a descriptive analysis of the data. How much time do CEOs spend at work versus on personal activities? How much do they spend in meetings versus thinking and reflecting alone? How much do they rely on email versus face-to-face conversation? Do they spend more time inside the company or outside, more with customers or investors? We'll answer those questions—and many more.

Second, we will offer prescriptions for how CEOs can manage their time more effectively across their many responsibilities. One of our most striking observations is that the way leaders allocate their time varies considerably. (See the exhibit "Looking beyond the averages.") Some of this variation reflects differences in their businesses and management practices. However, many time allocation decisions, such as participation in company rituals that offer limited return, reflect legacy norms and cultures, as well as a CEO's own habits. In our debriefings the CEOs all acknowledged that there were important areas where they could be using their time better. On the basis of these discussions and those with the hundreds of other CEOs in our workshops, we are convinced that every leader can improve his or her time management.

Finally, we will reflect on what our rich data reveals about the overall role of the CEO. A CEO has to simultaneously manage multiple dimensions of influence, which all contain dualities, or seeming contradictions, that effective CEOs must integrate. Understanding this broader view of the role is essential to success and also provides an important perspective for managing time well.

While our research focuses on the CEO role in large, complex companies, its findings have implications for all leaders (including executives of nonprofits) looking for ways to use their time and influence more effectively.

The Job Is All-Consuming

CEOs are always on, and there is always more to be done. The leaders in our study worked 9.7 hours per weekday, on average. They also conducted business on 79% of weekend days, putting in an average of 3.9 hours daily, and on 70% of vacation days, averaging 2.4 hours daily. As these figures show, the CEO's job is relentless.

About half (47%) of a CEO's work was done at company headquarters. The rest was conducted while visiting other company locations, meeting external constituencies, commuting, traveling, and at home. Altogether, the CEOs in our study worked an average of 62.5 hours a week.

Why such a grueling schedule? Because it is essential to the role. Every constituency associated with a company wants direct contact with the person at the top. As much as CEOs rely on delegation, they can't hand off everything. They have to spend at least some time with each constituency in order to provide direction, create alignment, win support, and gather the information needed to make good decisions. Travel is also an absolute must. You can't run a domestic company, let alone a global one, from headquarters alone. As a CEO, you have to be out and about.

Making time for personal well-being

Given that work could consume every hour of their lives, CEOs have to set limits so that they can preserve their health and their relationships with family and friends. Most of the CEOs in our study recognized that. They slept, on average, 6.9 hours a night, and many had regular exercise regimens, which consumed about 9% of their nonwork hours (or about 45 minutes a day). To sustain the intensity of the job, CEOs need to train—just as elite athletes do. That means allocating time for health, fitness, and rest.

We paid special attention to the 25% of time—or roughly six hours a day—when CEOs were awake and not working. Typically, they spent about half those hours with their families, and most had learned to become very disciplined about this. Most also found at least some hours (2.1 a day, on average) for downtime, which included everything from watching television and reading for pleasure to hobbies like photography.

The CEO's job is mentally and physically demanding. Activities that preserve elements of normal life keep CEOs grounded and better able to engage with colleagues and workers—as opposed to distant, detached, and disconnected. CEOs also have to make time for their own professional renewal and development (which our data showed was often the biggest casualty of a packed schedule). And they must be careful, as our colleague Tom DeLong puts it, not to become "like race car drivers and treat home like a pit stop."

They Work Face-to-Face

The top job in a company involves primarily face-to-face interactions, which took up 61% of the work time of the CEOs we studied. Another 15% was spent on the phone or reading and replying to written correspondence. The final 24% was spent on electronic communications.

Face-to-face interaction is the best way for CEOs to exercise influence, learn what's really going on, and delegate to move forward the multiple agendas that must be advanced. It also allows CEOs to best support and coach the people they work closely with. How a CEO spends face-to-face time is viewed as a signal of what or who is important; people watch this more carefully than most CEOs recognize.

Avoiding the lure of email

In theory, email helps leaders cut down on face-to-face meetings and improve productivity. In reality, many find it ineffective and a dangerous time sink—but one they have trouble avoiding. Email interrupts work, extends the workday, intrudes on time for family and thinking, and is not conducive to thoughtful discussions. CEOs are endlessly copied on FYI emails. They feel pressure to respond because ignoring an email seems rude.

CEOs should recognize that the majority of emails cover issues that needn't involve them and often draw them into the operational weeds. Conversely, emails from the CEO can create a downward spiral of unnecessary communication and set the wrong norms, especially if the CEO sends them late at night, on weekends, or on holidays. It then becomes easy for everyone in an organization to fall into the bad habit of overusing electronic communications.

That's why setting proper expectations and norms for what emails the CEO needs to receive—and when he or she will respond—is essential. Norms are necessary for the others in the organization as well, to prevent email from having a cascading effect on everyone, wasting precious hours and intruding on personal time. One way for the CEO to stay ahead of the digital avalanche is to have an adept EA filter messages and delegate many of them to others before the CEO even sees them. In the end, though, there is no substitute for being disciplined about resisting the siren call of electronic communications. This is a topic our CEOs were often animated about, and best practices in this area are still emerging.

Some CEOs in our study have begun to use videoconferencing as an alternative to face-to-face meetings, especially to cut down on travel for themselves and for team members who might otherwise have to come to see them. Although such efficiencies should surely be sought, CEOs must never forget that at its core their job is a face-to-face one.

They Are Agenda Driven

CEOs oversee a large number of organizational units and work streams and countless types of decisions. Our research finds that they should have an explicit personal agenda and that most do. A clear and effective agenda optimizes the CEO's limited time; without one, demands from the loudest constituencies will take over, and the most important work won't get done.

A good agenda sets priorities for the CEO's personal involvement over the coming period. But it is not unidimensional; rather, it is a matrix including both broader areas for improvement and specific matters that need to be addressed, and it combines time-bound goals with more open-ended priorities.

In our study we asked each CEO to describe the agenda he or she was pursuing during the quarter being tracked and to highlight the hours devoted primarily to advancing it. Every executive provided an agenda. We found that the CEOs invested significant time—43%, on average—in activities that furthered their agendas. Some were far more disciplined about this than others: Time devoted to the core agenda varied widely, ranging from 14% to 80% of leaders' work hours. Most CEOs we talked with agreed that the more time they spent on their agendas, the better they felt about their use of time.

Overall, we found that an explicit agenda is one of the CEO's most important tools for making progress on multiple work streams simultaneously, addressing differences in the rate of progress across priorities, and using time effectively despite the need to respond personally to unforeseen events.

Advancing the agenda
Keeping time allocation aligned with CEOs' top priorities is so crucial that we suggest that every quarter CEOs make a point of looking back at whether their schedule for the previous period adequately matched up with their personal agenda. They should also update the agenda to reflect current circumstances.

Four Behaviors of Great Executive Assistants

EXECUTIVE ASSISTANTS PLAY A VITAL ROLE in shielding CEOs from distractions and unnecessary activities and ensuring that leaders' limited time is used well. We often hear CEOs say that a highly skilled EA can dramatically increase their efficiency and effectiveness, and our research supports that view.

EAs often feel conflicting pressures, however, that can result in poor scheduling choices. For instance, although they may recognize that CEOs need time alone, our study shows that many EAs believe that a full CEO calendar signals that they're doing their job. They tend to book back-to-back appointments, limiting time for spontaneous communications or solitary reflection. In addition, while EAs recognize that protecting a CEO's time is one of their most important duties, some have a human reluctance to say no to people (especially colleagues in the organization). That allows unessential meetings to creep into the CEO's day. Conversely, other EAs take their traditional role as gatekeeper too far, maintaining such tight control over access that their bosses risk being seen as aloof or inaccessible.

Finding the right balance in managing the CEO's time requires judgment and emotional intelligence. It also requires strong communication skills, because an EA speaks for the CEO and can affect how a leader comes across. In our research we have identified four key behaviors that drive better performance:

1. **Understand the leader's agenda.** CEOs should have a written agenda detailing their top priorities (updated quarterly) and should spend much of their time on activities that advance the agenda. It's critical

---

CEOs can benefit from making their personal agenda explicit to others. Their EAs and leadership teams both need to know and understand it so that they can stay aligned with it. (See the sidebar "Four Behaviors of Great Executive Assistants.") This understanding will help team members assume ownership of the goals and priorities of the work the CEO needs them to drive.

Dealing with unfolding developments

A good portion of our CEOs' time (about 36%, on average) was spent in a reactive mode, handling unfolding issues, both internal and external. For many chief executives, it is not immediately clear when

that the EA internalize this agenda and use it as a lens through which each meeting request is viewed. The CEO's responsibility is to ensure that the EA knows the agenda and the importance of keeping the schedule aligned with it.

2. **Include all the relevant players.** Managers at all levels tend to complain about having too many meetings. One solution is to try keeping meetings small and inviting only those whose attendance is essential. However, good CEOs delegate well, and to do so they need their direct reports and affected managers to be present. Otherwise, extra rounds of communication and follow-up will be needed after meetings. Good EAs avoid that problem by getting the right players in the room to begin with.

3. **Recognize the value of spontaneity.** Most CEOs are overbooked. They would benefit from more time to walk the hallways and initiate unplanned interactions. They also need room to react to events that can't be anticipated; leaving some open time in the leader's day will help EAs avoid frequently canceling and rescheduling appointments.

4. **Zealously protect personal and family time.** EAs should recognize that the long hours, travel, and stress of the CEO job can take a toll. Time with family and friends, regular exercise, and opportunities to recharge and reflect are crucial to effectiveness and avoiding burnout. EAs' daily scheduling choices play an important part in helping CEOs maintain the balance they need to succeed over the long haul.

and how to address such issues or how much time to devote to them. Say that a member of the CEO's senior leadership team leaves a meeting looking upset. Should the CEO follow up with that person right away to make sure everything is OK? Should the CEO just wait and let the team member cool off? Sometimes emerging problems seem small at first but balloon into larger distractions if the CEO doesn't attend to them. In other instances a CEO's intervention makes an issue bigger than it might have been. It's essential for CEOs to figure out appropriate responses to these unfolding situations.

Every now and then, CEOs find themselves dealing with a sudden, full-blown crisis—a product or safety failure, a hostile activist's bid, a serious cyberattack, or even an external catastrophe such as a tsunami or a terrorist attack. Most of our CEOs (89%) spent some time on crises. Though on average it was small (1% of work time during the quarter we tracked), the total amount spent varied a great deal among the leaders in our study. Crises can create make-or-break moments in a CEO's leadership. In dealing with them, CEOs need to be highly visible and personally involved; the response to such events can't be delegated. Showing genuine concern for the people affected, avoiding defensiveness, holding everyone together, and creating confidence that the organization will not only survive but emerge stronger are some of the things CEOs need to do during these times.

Limiting routine responsibilities

A surprisingly significant fraction (11%, on average) of our CEOs' work time was consumed by routine duties. Such activities varied considerably across CEOs, running the gamut from review meetings to board meetings, earnings calls, and investor days.

Operating reviews are a major component of a CEO's routine tasks. Their number, frequency, and length ranged widely across the leaders we studied, and our discussions suggested that some CEOs—especially those who had been COOs—overinvested in reviews that could be delegated to direct reports.

The ability of CEOs to control what we term "have-to-dos" was also quite variable. Have-to-dos include rituals such as giving welcome talks to new employees. These can play an important symbolic role and help reinforce the company's values and culture. By thoughtfully choosing which of these events to attend, CEOs can set the tone of their relationship with the organization. Yet a CEO must be disciplined about ensuring that feel-good activities don't collectively take up more time than he or she can afford.

Our discussions suggest that CEOs need to take a hard look at every activity that falls into the routine and have-to-do categories. They must ask whether it serves an important purpose or is simply a company habit, something instituted by the predecessor, or a carry-over from the CEO's previous role.

They Rely Heavily on Their Direct Reports

A CEO's direct reports are the company's most senior executives and include some of its most skilled managers. They span all the key elements of the business and offer CEOs the greatest opportunity for leverage. The leadership team, working together, can be the glue that helps the CEO integrate the company and get the work done.

In our study about half (46%) of a CEO's time with internal constituencies was spent with one or more direct reports, and 21% of it was spent only with direct reports. The total time spent with direct reports ranged from a low of 32% of time with internal constituencies to a high of 67%. When we explored that variation, we found that CEOs were more likely to spend time with their reports present when they had greater confidence in them.

We found that it's critical for each member of the leadership team to have the capabilities to excel and earn the CEO's full trust and support. Any weaknesses in this group significantly reduce the CEO's effectiveness, because dealing with work that reports should have handled, and cleaning up after them, eats up valuable time. In fact, when our CEOs gathered as a group across cohorts to see how things were going after they had been in office awhile, their number one regret was not setting high-enough standards in selecting direct reports. Many CEOs told us this was because they focused too much on the present and not enough on the future when they first stepped into the role. Direct reports who could manage the status quo were often not the ones who could help the CEO take the company to a new level.

The more CEOs can delegate to their leadership team, the better they generally feel about their use of time. It eases the burden of needing to get personally engaged, following up, and asking others to report back. Since CEOs see their direct reports so frequently, it is also easy to stay in touch with how things are going with matters they are handling.

Staying connected to other managers

The CEOs in our study also spent considerable time (32% of their time with internal constituencies, on average) with a broader group of senior leaders, often called the top 100 (plus or minus). Many in this group report to the CEO's direct reports. We found that time with this next level of leadership was well spent. The top 100 are often the driving force for execution in the organization, and direct contact with the CEO can help align and motivate them. These leaders are also key to succession planning: Some will be candidates to replace the company's most senior executives. Given that the people at this level are often a generation younger, a few may eventually even be candidates to succeed the CEO. So getting to know them personally can be very useful.

Not surprisingly, the CEOs in our study spent less time with lower-level managers (14%, on average) and even less time with rank-and-file employees (about 6%, on average). However, our research suggests that effective CEOs need to be careful to maintain a human face in the organization. They must stay approachable and find ways to meaningfully engage with employees at all levels. This not only keeps them in touch with what is really going on in the company but helps them model and communicate organizational values throughout the workforce.

Direct human contact with the rank and file also grounds CEOs and helps them understand employees' reality. CEOs face a real risk of operating in a bubble and never seeing the actual world their workers face. Relationships with employees at multiple levels also build a CEO's legitimacy and trustworthiness in the eyes of employees, which is essential to motivating them and winning their support.

Knowing what is going on

Spending time with the rank and file, and with savvy external frontline constituencies, is also an indispensable way to gain reliable information on what is really going on in the company and in the industry. This is a major CEO challenge. Some CEOs get frontline contact by walking the hallways and factory floors, and using mechanisms like periodic lunches, unscheduled visits, and carefully designed field trips to customer and company sites. Others use group interactions, such as town halls, to foster genuine and open conversations with a large cross section of employees (rather than present slide decks). Our data indicates that CEOs have varying success in carving out time for such steps, however.

They Manage Using Broad Integrating Mechanisms

CEOs must avoid trying to do too much themselves. It just isn't possible for them to make or even ratify most decisions directly. Instead, effective CEOs put in place well-designed structures and processes that help everyone else in the organization make good choices. These inform, support, enable, and integrate the work of others while building the organization's capabilities.

The most powerful integrating mechanisms include strategy (on which CEOs in our study spent an average of 21% of their work time), functional and business unit reviews (25% of their time), developing people and relationships (25% of their time), matching organizational structure and culture with the needs of the business (16% of their time), and mergers and acquisitions (4% of their time).

Harnessing strategy

The CEO's single most powerful lever is ensuring that every unit—and the company as a whole—has a clear, well-defined strategy. Strategy creates alignment among the many decisions within a business and across the organization. By spending time on strategy, a CEO provides direction for the company, helps make its value proposition explicit, and defines how it will compete in the marketplace and differentiate itself from rivals. Strategy also provides clarity on what the company will *not* do. A compelling strategy—if well understood throughout the organization—is motivating and energizing. And without clarity on strategy, the CEO will be drawn into too many tactical decisions.

In large, complex firms, CEOs can almost never spend enough time on strategy—they must constantly be working to shape it, refine it, communicate it, reinforce it, and help people recognize when they may be drifting from it. CEOs must also ensure that the strategy is renewed from time to time and based on changes in the environment. Portfolio choices such as divestitures, mergers, and acquisitions are critical to strategy, and a CEO must be personally involved with them.

Aligning organizational structure and culture

To foster appropriate decisions across the company, the organization's structure needs to be aligned with its strategy. Otherwise, the CEO will be drawn into endless adjudication among units. It can also become a big drain on the CEO and others if the organization is constantly lurching from one structure to another.

Culture—which encompasses an organization's values, beliefs, and norms—is another key CEO lever for reinforcing strategy and influencing how the organization as a whole goes about doing its work. CEOs can shape a company's culture in many ways, from the time they spend talking about it at various forums, to personally living the valued behaviors, to recognizing, rewarding, and celebrating those who exemplify the desired culture while taking corrective action with those who don't. It is the CEO's job to champion the organization's culture and constantly look for opportunities to strengthen it.

Designing, monitoring, and improving processes

CEOs must ensure that the company's strategy is being well executed. This will occur when the organization has rigorous processes through which work—such as marketing plans, pricing, product development, and strategy development itself—is done. Good processes bring together the best organizational knowledge and keep the CEO from continually having to override decisions.

Formal reviews are essential to monitoring whether the company is delivering the required process performance. Though these consume a quarter of a CEO's total work time, they allow CEOs to track progress, provide regular feedback, uphold high standards, and ensure timely course corrections. Reviews are also necessary to make sure that lessons learned are used to enhance the various processes through which work gets done.

However, excessive participation in reviews can get the CEO too involved in the company's operations and mired in unnecessary details. We talked a lot with the CEOs in our study about this problem. We have found, again and again, that many have a hard time shedding the COO or president roles they may have previously held.

Some also forget that their senior team should bear the primary responsibility for many reviews and keep the CEO informed on a regular basis.

When CEOs fail to delegate reviews to direct reports who can handle them, they erode the autonomy and accountability of their management teams. That doesn't help CEOs get the best out of others.

Developing people and relationships

Building the company's leadership pipeline is an important CEO function in its own right. We have found that CEOs must be personally committed to and be involved in improving the quality of the company's leaders. They cannot just leave this task to HR. Leadership choices are also pivotal in shaping the company's culture. Who gets hired, promoted, or fired signals what is truly valued by the CEO and the company.

CEOs need to get the most out of an organization's talent, and to do that, they must forge personal connections. Our CEOs spent another quarter of their total work time in meetings that focused on building relationships. When trust is mutual, delegation comes more naturally, agreement is easier to reach, and less monitoring and follow-up are necessary. Good relationships also make people more likely to give you the benefit of the doubt when you need it— and to tell you the truth, which is invaluable at the top.

The time CEOs spend building social capital through a network of personal relationships has many benefits and is time well spent.

They Are Always in Meetings

CEOs attend an endless stream of meetings, each of which can be totally different from the one before and the one that follows. Their sheer number and variety is a defining feature of the top job. On average, the leaders in our study had 37 meetings of assorted lengths in any given week and spent 72% of their total work time in meetings.

Looking beyond the averages

How much do CEOs' practices differ? We've ranked the variation in their uses of time from the lowest to the highest.

	Degree of variation (standard deviation/mean)	
Meeting time	0.14	
Face-to-face interactions	0.14	
Time with internal constituencies	0.14	
Total workweek obligations	0.14	
One-hour meetings	0.21	Low
Scheduled time	0.22	
One-on-one meetings	0.24	
CEO-initiated meetings	0.28	
Weekend days worked	0.31	
Core agenda time	0.36	
Meetings per week	0.36	
Electronic communication	0.38	
Time with direct reports	0.39	
Functional and business-unit review time	0.41	Medium
People and relationship time	0.44	
Strategy time	0.48	
Time on organizational structure and culture	0.54	
Spontaneous time	0.59	
Have-to-do time	0.59	
Time with other outside commitments	0.59	
Two-hour-plus blocks of alone time	0.70	High
Time with rank-and-file employees	0.71	
Exercise time	0.89	
Time with investors	0.95	
Time with customers	1.10	

Making meetings shorter and more effective

CEOs need to regularly review which meetings are truly needed and which can be delegated, and to let go of ones they were accustomed to in previous roles.

They should also take a hard look at meeting length. In our study, meetings that lasted an hour accounted for 32% of a CEO's meetings, on average. Meetings that were longer accounted for 38%, and shorter meetings, 30%. We found that the length of meetings was often a matter of organizational or personal habit or both—a default length (like one hour) was the norm.

"Standard" meeting times should be revisited with an eye toward shortening them. Doing this can significantly enhance a CEO's efficiency. In our debriefs, CEOs confessed that one-hour meetings could often be cut to 30 or even 15 minutes. Another good way to streamline things is to reset meeting norms: Every meeting should have a clear agenda, and to minimize repetition, attendees should come prepared. Effective CEOs spread these meeting norms throughout the organization.

Some CEOs were worried that they might appear standoffish if someone asked for an hour and the CEO (or the EA) offered 30 minutes. But we have found that meeting length is worth confronting. "Whatever they ask for, cut it in half," said one CEO.

Another important meeting attribute is the number and composition of attendees. One-on-one meetings were the most common (accounting for 42% of CEOs' meetings, on average), followed by meetings with two to five participants (21%). Although every CEO had meetings involving large groups of 50 or more—like town halls, leadership off-sites, or all-company meetings—these were infrequent (5% of meetings).

The emphasis on one-on-one and small group meetings makes sense for enabling delegation and relationship building, and allows confidentiality. But leaders should also look for opportunities to bring the right people together. An essential part of the CEO's role is to align various internal and external constituencies around a common understanding of issues, decisions, and action agendas. Having the right people in the room is a powerful way to build that alignment and avoid the need for repetitive, time-consuming interactions to bring everyone along.

Allowing for accessibility and spontaneity

The vast majority of our CEOs' time (75%, on average) was scheduled in advance. The CEOs initiated more than half (51%) of their meetings themselves.

While controlling the nature and number of meetings is essential, we also found that CEOs need to regularly set aside time for more spontaneous interaction (which represented 25% of their work time in our study). This frees up space for same-day appointments initiated by others, for opportune conversations or meetings, and for responding to unfolding events.

The amount of time our CEOs allowed for spontaneous meetings varied considerably, ranging from 3% to 61%. In our debriefings, CEOs who discovered that they had left little room for spur-of-the-moment meetings were often surprised and quick to recognize the need for change.

Spontaneity and accessibility enhance a CEO's legitimacy. Leaders whose schedules are always booked up or whose EAs see themselves as gatekeepers and say no to too many people risk being viewed as imperious, self-important, or out of touch. EAs play a key role in finding the right balance here.

Carving out alone time

It's also vital for CEOs to schedule adequate uninterrupted time by themselves so that they can have space to reflect and prepare for meetings. In our study, CEOs spent 28% of their work time alone, on average—but again, that varied a great deal, from a low of 10% to a high of 48%. Unfortunately, too much of this alone time (59% of it) was fragmented into blocks of an hour or less; too little (18%) was in blocks of two hours or longer. CEOs need to cordon off meaningful amounts of alone time and avoid dissipating it by dealing with immediate matters, especially their in-boxes. This proved to be a common problem among the CEOs in our study, who readily acknowledged it.

Given that time in the office is easily eaten up, alone time outside the office is particularly beneficial. Long-distance travel out of contact with the office often provides critical thinking time, and many CEOs swear by it. To capitalize on it, CEOs should avoid traveling with an entourage.

They Juggle Many External Constituencies

While the CEOs we studied spent the majority of their time (70%, on average) dealing with internal constituencies, a good chunk (30%, on average) was spent with outsiders: 16% with business partners (such as customers, suppliers, bankers, investors, consultants, lawyers, PR firms, and other service providers), 5% with the company's board of directors, and 9% on other outside commitments (service on other boards, industry groups, dealing with the media and the government, and community and philanthropic activities).

External constituencies can be just as demanding as internal ones. Everyone wants to talk to the CEO, and dealing with external stakeholders is time-consuming. It often involves longer workdays and time away from headquarters and from home. There is a risk of drifting toward outside commitments less tied to company success.

Finding time for customers

Most of our CEOs were dismayed to discover how little time they spent with their customers—just 3%, on average. It surprised some even more to learn that this was less than the amount they spent with consultants. The scant time devoted to customers is partly a function of the huge scope of internal responsibilities: As an executive ascends from managing a line of business (which involves more-frequent customer contact) to the job of leading the entire company, it is natural for customer-facing time to decline.

Nonetheless, the CEOs in our study clearly felt that 3% was too low. Customers are a key source of independent information about the company's progress, industry trends, and competitors. In the B2B space, meeting with customers' CEOs is highly valuable, since peer conversations can be very candid. In B2C companies, there are also rich opportunities for customer contact. For retail CEOs, for example, store visits—especially unannounced ones—are an indispensable way to talk to regular customers, not just the company staff.

Some CEOs systematically schedule time with customers. The CEO of a financial services firm in our study, for instance, aims to meet face-to-face with one customer a day. A manufacturing CEO allocates two days a month to customer visits. Other CEOs try to build customer visits into their travel. A habit of some type seems to be the most reliable way to ensure enough customer time.

Limiting time with investors

On average, our CEOs spent only 3% of their total work time on investors. Most of them found this surprising; they tended to believe they spent more. But while more time is likely to be better when it comes to customers, the same is not true with investors. Too many meetings with investors can easily become a time sink and can draw the CEO into trying to manage the stock price rather than focusing on business fundamentals. Staying in touch with a few key buy-side investors, doing quarterly calls, and holding an annual investor day may be all a CEO needs to do—unless, of course, the company is dealing with serious investor unrest or activism. By and large, the CEOs in our study seem to have discovered such focus over time, after getting caught up early in their tenures in too much investor relations.

Limiting unrelated outside commitments

There is a real risk that CEOs will get distracted by outside activities not directly connected to the business, where they are in high demand and which often involve worthy community and social issues. Such activities consumed an average of almost 2% of the work time of the CEOs in our study. While CEOs should give back to their communities and play the role of business statespeople, they should carefully restrict the hours they personally spend on such activities and on participating in business groups. Though the CEO's presence can be important, overseeing and managing such work does not require the CEO and can be delegated to direct reports, for whom it is motivational and provides professional development opportunities.

Finding time for directors

All our CEOs understood the importance of spending time with their boards. In our study, interacting with directors accounted for 5% of CEOs' total work time, or 41 hours a quarter, on average. But again we saw significant variation: One CEO spent six hours with directors; another spent 165.

A CEO must never forget that the board is his or her boss and that "managing up" is vital to success. However, that involves more than board meetings, committee meetings, and board retreats; CEOs must find time to build meaningful one-on-one relationships with individual directors. This is essential to take advantage of each board member's particular expertise and perspective. At board meetings, it's often not clear where each director is coming from, but that knowledge is crucial in crises and when dealing with controversial topics. CEOs also need to keep the directors well informed and engage with them between meetings through newsletters and updates. A common understanding and alignment with the board is important in periods of stress or market challenge.

Dimensions of the CEO's Role and Influence

The data on CEOs' time use reveals that the sheer complexity of their role—the myriad types of work, activities, and constituencies— is much greater than has previously been documented or perhaps even understood.

In examining the CEO's role, we have come to see that their work entails six dimensions of influence. Each involves a duality—a seeming contradiction, akin to yin and yang—that CEOs must manage simultaneously in order to be effective. (See the exhibit "Managing the dimensions of CEO influence.")

First, CEOs clearly have *direct* influence over many issues and decisions, as their numerous reviews and one-on-one meetings reveal. However, the inherent limits on CEOs' time and knowledge

Managing the dimensions of CEO influence

Chief executives exert influence along six dimensions, each of which involves a duality, or seeming contradiction akin to yin and yang. Managing these dualities simultaneously is a hallmark of effective CEOs.

Direct

The CEO is directly involved in numerous agendas and makes many decisions.

Indirect

The CEO also exerts much influence over the work of others, using integrative mechanisms, processes, structures, and norms.

Internal

The CEO works with the senior team and with employees at all other levels to get all the organization's work done.

External

The CEO also engages myriad external constituencies, serving as the face of the company, and must bring these external perspectives to the organization.

Proactive

The CEO must articulate a sense of purpose, have a forward-looking vision, and lead the company to greater success.

Reactive

The CEO must also respond to events as they unfold, from daily issues to full-blown crises that will prove to have a major impact on the company's success.

Leverage

CEOs' position and control of resources give them immense clout.

Constraints

CEOs are constrained by the need to build buy-in, bring others along, and send the right message.

Tangible

The CEO makes many decisions about concrete things like strategic direction, structure, resource allocation, and the selection of key people.

Symbolic

Much of CEOs' influence proves to be intangible and symbolic; their actions set the tone, communicate norms, shape values, and provide meaning.

Power

CEOs hold formal power and authority in the company that is reinforced by their competence and track record.

Legitimacy

CEOs' influence also rests on legitimacy that comes from their character and the trust they earn from employees through their demonstrated values, fairness, and commitment to the organization.

mean that much of their influence must also be *indirect*. Good CEOs are very much in charge but work through others using strategy, culture, and effective organizational processes that drive sound analysis and alignment across the organization. CEOs need to learn how to marry direct and indirect influence.

Second, much of a CEO's work necessarily involves *internal* constituencies and managerial tasks, and our data verifies the overwhelming amount of such work to be done. However, CEOs are unique in the degree to which they must also engage and influence numerous *external* constituencies and represent the company to the world. Effective CEOs connect their internal and external roles by bringing outside perspectives into the work of the company. They also need to make sure outside constituencies understand the company's work and value.

Third, much of a CEO's work is inherently *proactive*: It involves anticipating problems, gathering the facts, conducting analyses, and making sound and timely choices. Here, the CEO sets and drives the agenda. However, *reacting* well to unplanned and unforeseen events and crises is some of the most important work CEOs do. Choices here, and the CEO's personal presence or lack of presence, can have major consequences both outside and within the organization. Such periods can make or break a company and the CEO's own capacity to lead.

Fourth, while CEOs have a great deal of *leverage* to exert because of their position in the hierarchy and access to resources, they also face numerous—and often unrecognized—*constraints* and complexities in exercising that leverage. They are constrained in how often they can overturn decisions that have been brought to them for approval or how quickly they can drive changes without securing the support and buy-in of their senior team and board of directors. They must identify the group or people who are needed to bring about a change and then figure out how to win over the leader that will mobilize them. CEOs must find the right balance between taking full advantage of the leverage they possess, while being equally sensitive to the constraints they must navigate and the constituencies they must bring along. Otherwise, resistance will emerge and come back to bite them.

Fifth, while much of the CEO's influence is highly *tangible,* involving decisions about things like strategic priorities, budget targets, and people selection, some of the CEO's greatest influence is *symbolic.* This comes from the meaning people attach to a CEO's actions. What CEOs do (and don't do), including everyday things like how they dress, what cars they drive, where they park, where they eat, and whom they talk to and how—always sends implicit messages to the company and its constituencies. Everything a CEO does affects what the organization focuses on, its norms of behavior, and its culture and values. The symbolic effects of CEOs' choices can reach even further than their specific actions.

Sixth, CEOs hold a great deal of formal *power* and authority, and exercise it in the many ways we have described. However, power, authority, competence, and even results are insufficient to truly ensure their success. Effective CEOs combine formal power and authority with *legitimacy.* CEOs achieve legitimacy when employees believe in them as people and as leaders. They earn legitimacy in multiple ways—by demonstrating values, ethics, fairness, and a selfless commitment to the company and its people, among other things. Legitimacy gives rise to motivation that goes far beyond carrying out orders and can lead to extraordinary organizational performance. CEO time allocation, then, is not simply a matter of what

What Do CEOs Actually Do?

WHILE WE REALIZE THAT CORPORATE leaders are really busy, we know surprisingly little about their day-to-day schedules. To fill that gap, in 2006 Harvard Business School professors Michael Porter and Nitin Nohria began asking participants of their New CEO Workshop to track their use of time, 24/7, for 13 weeks. The data on these pages, which were created with assistance from Harvard Business School research associate Sarah Higgins, summarizes the information gathered on how 27 CEOs spent a total of nearly 60,000 hours. Here is how they allocated their time, on average, among various activities, places, priorities, meetings, and constituencies.

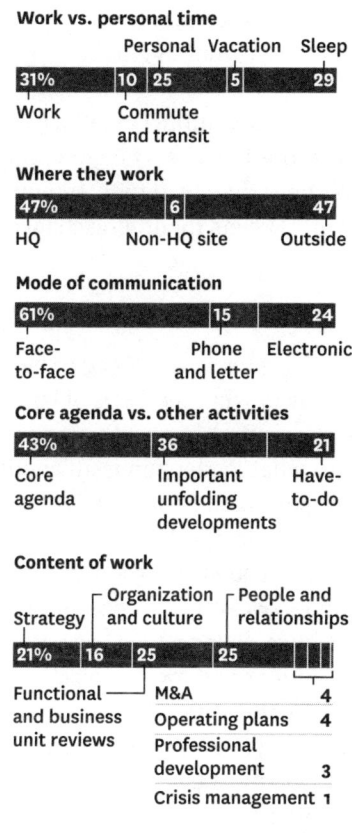

Work vs. personal time

	Personal	Vacation	Sleep
31%	10	25	5	29

Work · Commute and transit

Where they work

47%	6	47

HQ · Non-HQ site · Outside

Mode of communication

61%	15	24

Face-to-face · Phone and letter · Electronic

Core agenda vs. other activities

43%	36	21

Core agenda · Important unfolding developments · Have-to-do

Content of work

Strategy | Organization and culture | People and relationships

21%	16	25	25	

Functional and business unit reviews — M&A 4
Operating plans 4
Professional development 3
Crisis management 1

Length of meetings

	30m		1–2h		>5h
7%	23	32	21	13	4

<15m · 1h · 2–5h

Scheduled vs. spontaneous time

75%	25

Scheduled · Spontaneous

Meetings vs. alone time

72%	28

Meeting time · Alone time

Time with key constituencies

Insiders		Business partners	
Direct reports	33	Consultants	5
		Customers	3
Other senior managers	22	Investors	3
		Bankers	2
Other managers	10	Suppliers	1
		Legal/accounting	1
Other employees	5	Other	1

Board	
Full board	2
Individual board members	2
Committees	1

70%	16	9	5

Other outside commitments

Industry groups	5
Philanthopy	2
Media	1
Government/regulators	1

happens in meetings and decision-making processes. It reflects the far broader set of ways in which the CEO as an individual engages with the organization and its people.

In managing across these six dimensions of influence, it is easy for CEOs to overlook the less direct, less top-down, less tangible, and more human aspects of their work. Without this awareness, though, CEOs give up some of their most powerful levers for driving change.

Why Good Leaders Matter

Countless concepts, tools, and metrics have been developed to help leaders manage well. However, our study of what the CEOs of large, complex organizations actually do—as manifest in how they spend their time—opens a new window into what leadership is all about and into its many components and dimensions. Being the CEO is a highly challenging role, and it is difficult to do it well.

The success of CEOs has enormous consequences—good or bad—for employees, customers, communities, wealth creation, and the trajectory of economies and even societies. Being a CEO has gotten harder as the size and scope of the job continue to grow, organizational complexity rises, technology advances, competition increases, and CEO accountability intensifies. The ideas we have introduced here aim to provide current and future leaders, who must bear this enormous responsibility, with a broader understanding of their role and how to best use their most important resource: their time.

Originally published in July–August 2018. Reprint R1804B

The Best Leaders Are Great Teachers

by Sydney Finkelstein

KUNDAPUR VAMAN KAMATH WAS A TEACHER. But he didn't work at a school or stand in front of a class. Instead, he delivered his lessons at the office—to the employees who served under him during his four decades as a senior executive at, and then CEO of, India's ICICI Bank. Whether he was offering tips on stakeholder communication or explaining the importance of ambitious goals, Kamath treated each day as an opportunity to provide his direct reports with a customized master class in management. Over time, this approach transformed the company into a hothouse of leadership talent, accelerating its growth. ICICI became one of India's largest, most innovative banks, and Kamath has been credited with molding a whole generation of the country's banking executives.

I've spent more than 10 years studying world-class leaders like Kamath to determine what sets them apart from typical leaders. One big surprise was the extent to which these star managers emphasize ongoing, intensive one-on-one tutoring of their direct reports, either in person or virtually, in the course of daily work. Cognitive psychologists, teachers, and educational consultants have long recognized the value of such personalized instruction: It fosters not just competence or compliance but mastery of skills and independence of thought and action. However, it's unusual to see this type of teaching employed in a business context. Indeed, I've found that most leaders fall back on more-traditional employee management and development practices, such as giving formal reviews, making professional introductions, advising on career plans, acting as sounding boards, and helping to navigate internal politics. Although some managers do occasionally find themselves imparting a lesson or two, few give it much thought or make it a core part of their job.

By contrast, the exceptional leaders I studied were teachers through and through. They routinely spent time in the trenches with employees, passing on technical skills, general tactics, business principles, and life lessons. Their teaching was informal and organic, flowing out of the tasks at hand. And it had an unmistakable impact: Their teams and organizations were some of the highest-performing in their sectors.

Fortunately, it doesn't take special talent or training or even a lot of time to teach in the same way that star managers do. Simply follow the precedent they've set. Learn what to teach, when to teach, and how to make your lessons stick.

Unforgettable Lessons

Great leaders teach on a range of topics, but their best lessons—so relevant and useful that direct reports are often still applying and sharing them years later—fall into three buckets:

Professionalism

A manager who worked for real estate CEO and investor Bill Sanders told me that Sanders often gave advice on conducting oneself professionally. He explained how to effectively prepare for meetings, how to communicate a vision when attempting to sell, and how to look at the industry not as it is but as it could become. Protégés of Kamath have said that he showed them how to mentor subordinates in an appropriate and constructive manner—guiding them while still respecting their independence. Other managers spoke of learning from their leaders the value of emphasizing integrity and high ethical standards. "He started with credibility," former Burger King CEO Jeff Campbell said of the late Norman Brinker, a legend in fast casual dining and one of Campbell's early bosses. "It's clear that he really

Idea in Brief

What sets exceptional business leaders apart? One thing, says Sydney Finkelstein, is their ongoing commitment to giving direct reports one-on-one instruction. Finkelstein, a management professor at Dartmouth's Tuck School of Business, has studied world-class leaders for more than a decade. He's found that they make a point of personally imparting memorable lessons that fall into three categories: pointers on professionalism, technical knowledge and skills, and broader life lessons.

Finkelstein notes that when and where top leaders teach is almost as important as what they teach. Instead of waiting for formal reviews, great managers stay accessible to their employees and share their wisdom as opportune

moments arise, whether that's in the office or outside it. They also create teaching moments—often by taking protégés off-site.

How do they make lessons stick? Their techniques include

1. Customizing instruction to the needs, personality, and development path of each individual

2. Asking pertinent questions to deepen learning

3. Modeling the behavior they want others to practice

Finkelstein discusses numerous superstar leaders who are revered as great teachers and suggests that if you follow their example, you can strengthen your staff and drive superior business performance.

cared about how guests felt and what kind of people he had working for him." An executive who reported to Tommy Frist Jr. when he was the CEO of Hospital Corporation of America (HCA) recounted that Frist sometimes lectured doctors about the need to put patients first. "Your duty," he would tell them, "is to do just what you learned when you took the oath. If you ever have a business manager call you and encourage you to do something different from what you think is right, you call me, because the day we start doing that, we start shutting hospitals."

Points of craft

You might think that the most senior leaders would leave instruction about the nuts and bolts of their business to others. But stars like former hedge fund CEO Julian Robertson and fashion icon

Ralph Lauren trained their people in the same highly disciplined approach that they employed themselves—one rooted in extensive knowledge and experience. As a direct report said of Robertson, he "could, at any given time, know so much about so many different companies that an average person's head would spin." Mindy Grossman, CEO of Weight Watchers and a former executive at Polo Ralph Lauren, remembered standing in showrooms with Lauren and listening to him explain how to achieve authenticity and integrity in fashion whether they were "creating a $24 T-shirt or a $6,000 crocodile skirt." Similarly, employees who worked at Oracle under Larry Ellison noted that when he was running the company, he constantly shared his technical knowledge of software architecture. And Jim Sinegal, cofounder and retired CEO of Costco Wholesale, recalled the way his former boss, Price Club founder Sol Price, routinely tried to build his employees' expertise in the details of retailing: "We were tested every day, and if something wasn't done properly, he'd be certain to show us how to do it."

Life lessons

Of course, great leaders don't limit themselves to teaching about work—they also proffer deeper wisdom about life. That might seem like overstepping, but I discovered that managers found it extremely helpful. For example, an HCA physician interviewed by my research team remembered his former boss Frist showing him a note card on which he had written his near-term goals, intermediate-term goals, and long-term goals. In a lesson the doctor never forgot, Frist explained that he refined those goals each day and was surprised that more people didn't perform such an exercise.

Another example comes from Mike Gamson, a senior vice president at LinkedIn, who told *Business Insider* that his first meeting with the company's new CEO, Jeff Weiner, involved a two-hour discussion of Buddhist principles. Gamson said he wanted to be a more empathetic leader, and Weiner asked why he wasn't instead aiming to be more compassionate. The pair explored the difference between those concepts, with recourse to a religious parable. Gamson came to see that both types of leaders understand other people's perspectives. However, managers who empathize run the risk of getting drawn into the emotions of situations, whereas compassionate leaders are more likely to remain calm and clearheaded and thus more capable of rendering assistance. That lesson from Weiner changed Gamson's entire leadership philosophy.

Perfect Timing

When leaders teach is almost as important as what they teach. The successful leaders I studied didn't wait for formal reviews or even check-ins. They seized and created opportunities to impart wisdom.

On the job

When Sinegal was working with Price at Price Club, he knew that lessons could come at any time. According to Sinegal, Price "spent day and night teaching," whether giving advice on retail tactics or discussing how to be a better manager. Chase Coleman III, a protégé of Robertson's, said that Robertson was similarly "out to teach you a lesson" in every interaction, showing "how to do things and how to run a business."

Some leaders ensure on-the-job learning by working in open offices that allow them to observe employees, project accessibility, and encourage frequent conversations. Others opt for more-conventional offices but make a point of maintaining open-door policies and spending lots of time circulating among their staff, which means they can offer lessons on the spur of the moment—when people can best process and embrace them. A good example of this was relayed to me by Campbell, the Brinker disciple. One evening at the office, Brinker brought up a memo Campbell had recently sent to a team member directing him in some detail to take a specific action. "You know," Campbell vividly recalled his boss saying, "this is a thought for you: The next time you're going to tell someone like Bill to do something, try to give him the objective and leave it up to him to figure out how to do it. You'll find out how smart he is or isn't, and he'll probably come up with some things that you wouldn't have thought of yourself."

In manufactured moments

Great leaders don't wait for the "perfect" opening. They create teaching moments—often by taking protégés out of the office environment to more-relaxed settings or unusual places. Frist, an avid pilot, sometimes invited people up in his plane. Longtime *Philadelphia Inquirer* executive editor Gene Roberts would treat his direct reports to dinner and offer "little hints" on how to handle certain situations, one employee recalled. They were the "best seminar you could ever have," another Roberts-trained manager told me. An ICICI executive who often caught rides home from the office with Kamath discovered that this was one of his boss's favorite times to teach. Kamath would welcome all kinds of questions and offer reflections on everything from his business philosophy to his personal spirituality.

Famed chef and foodie entrepreneur René Redzepi, co-owner of the restaurant Noma in Copenhagen, takes off-site teaching to an extreme. In 2012 he relocated his entire staff to London to create a 10-day pop-up establishment. A few years later, the team members went to Tokyo for two months. The next year they moved to Sydney, Australia, for 10 weeks, and in 2017 they ran a pop-up in Tulum, Mexico, for seven weeks. The goal, Redzepi explained, was "to learn by exploring a different place and meeting new people." He took personal responsibility for ensuring that everyone was broadening his or her culinary horizons. Back home, he said, he and the staff worked "to apply all these new learnings to the everyday routine."

Expert Delivery

No matter when or where they chose to teach their lessons, the leaders I studied were smart enough not to pompously pontificate or pummel employees with too much information. They deployed these more-nuanced techniques:

Customized instruction

Best-in-class educators embrace personalization, tailoring lessons and support to match students' individual learning profiles. And great business leaders do the same thing. They know that each subordinate should be taught in a way that suits his or her particular needs, personality, and developmental trajectory. Craigslist founder Craig Newmark remembered getting that type of targeted advice from his former boss at a local IBM branch office after an incident in which he behaved like a know-it-all. Pulling him aside, his boss quietly said, "Don't correct people when it matters little."

A senior manager who worked for Sanders described a similar encounter. The man had used the phrase "you guys" in an important—and successful—meeting with potential business partners. Afterward, in private, Sanders chastised him for the informal language. "He put his arm around me like a father," the executive recalled, and made it clear that as good as the meeting was, "it could have been even better." He has since made a point of expunging "you guys" from his business vocabulary.

Robertson was a master at delivering targeted advice and, more generally, at customizing his ongoing interactions with protégés. "He was very good at understanding what motivated people and how to extract maximum performance out of them," Coleman explained. "For some people, it was by encouraging them, and for other people, it was by making them feel less comfortable. He would tailor his approach based on what he thought would be most effective."

Questions

Star leaders also take a page from Socrates and teach by asking sharp, relevant questions, often in the course of furthering their own learning. According to a colleague at HCA, Frist "was always asking probing questions to find out what was happening." He did it to "educate himself, not to make you feel like you were doing something appropriate or inappropriate. It was an educational venture."

Restaurateur Brinker likewise "was always asking questions," said a former senior executive who reported to him. "'What do you think about this? What do you think about that? If this were your restaurant, what would you do differently?' He pushed his people to do the same thing: 'Have you talked to employees? What kind of guest feedback do you have?'"

Modeling

Another powerful and common teaching tactic deployed by executives I studied, used in conjunction with the other techniques I've mentioned, was the simplest: leading by example. Andrew Golden, president of the Princeton University Investment Company, reported that his former boss, Yale's chief investment officer David Swensen, was known for assuring ambitious new hires that he would do everything he could to help them not only develop but also move on to new jobs when they were ready—which is exactly how Golden ended up in his current role. He and other Swensen disciples learned the strategy by watching Swensen employ it, and now they practice it themselves. "It's a great recruiting tool," Golden noted.

One of Frist's direct reports told me that he learned how "to be a lot more adventurous" just by being around Frist, who was "incredibly creative in how the company was built and put together." Another Frist manager commented: "You learned as much from watching Tommy" as you did from listening to him. Sometimes, just seeing the right example in front of you is all it takes to pick up new behaviors.

Ultimately, great leaders understand that even a little bit of high-quality, one-on-one teaching can yield great dividends. As the boss, you command your employees' attention, and the lessons you impart will be more relevant, better-timed, and more personalized than content delivered in traditional leadership-training programs. And when you embrace the role of teacher, you build loyalty, turbocharge your team's development, and drive superior business performance.

Teaching is not merely an "extra" for good managers; it's an integral responsibility. If you're not teaching, you're not really leading.

Originally published in January–February 2018. Reprint R1801M

Nimble Leadership

by Deborah Ancona, Elaine Backman, and Kate Isaacs

NOBODY HAS REALLY *RECOMMENDED* command-and-control leadership for a long time. But no fully formed alternative has emerged, either. That's partly because high-level executives are ambivalent about changing their own behavior. They know perfectly well that their companies need to become more innovative—and they suspect it won't happen unless they're willing to push power, decision making, and resource allocation lower in the organization. But they're terrified that the business will fall into chaos if they loosen the reins.

In our research at MIT we've sought to understand how that tension gets resolved in organizations with a strong track record of continuous innovation. Most studies of leadership in fast-changing, uncertain environments have focused either on traditional bureaucracies attempting to become more agile or on very young, entrepreneurial companies. We took a different tack, looking in depth at two organizations that have been around a long time—and therefore have frequently adjusted to changing conditions—and have also maintained an entrepreneurial spirit and a first-class innovation capability: PARC, Xerox's famous R&D company in Silicon Valley, and W.L. Gore & Associates, the privately held materials science company.

During several rounds of qualitative data collection and follow-up interviews from 2009 to 2011 (with updates in 2019), we found many processes and behaviors commonly associated with agile organizations: multidisciplinary teams, a spirit of experimentation, and so forth. But we saw less familiar patterns of leadership, too.

First, we identified three distinct types of leaders. *Entrepreneurial leaders,* typically concentrated at lower levels of an organization, create value for customers with new products and services; collectively, they move the organization into unexplored territory. *Enabling leaders,* in the middle of the organization, make sure the entrepreneurs have the resources and information they need. And *architecting leaders,* near the top, keep an eye on the whole game board, monitoring culture, high-level strategy, and structure.

Second, both PARC and Gore integrate cultural norms—many dating back to their earliest days—that support innovation and resilience. The most important of these might be a shared belief that "leadership" should rest with whoever is best positioned to exercise it, regardless of title.

The three leadership roles, along with the cultural norms, have allowed the two organizations to become self-managing to a surprising degree. Many employees define and choose their own work assignments. New products and services are dreamed up not by high-level strategists or "innovators" housed in a separate incubator but by teams of employees who are free to walk away if a project loses steam. Early-stage funding goes to the projects that attract staffing; as success escalates, more resources flow in. And because lots of small bets are being made and employees are choosing which ones to back—that is, which project teams to join—the companies themselves become collective prediction markets that pool talent around good ideas and drain it from bad ones.

And here's the real beauty of the system: The mechanisms that enable self-management also balance freedom and control. The companies function efficiently and exploit new opportunities quickly even as they minimize bureaucratic rules.

Let's look first at the three types of leaders and the cultural norms they embody.

Idea In Brief

The Challenge

Mature companies struggle to balance the need for innovation (which requires creative self-starters at all levels of the organization) with the need for discipline (which calls for strong internal controls).

The Case Studies

PARC and W.L. Gore are exceptions. They've held onto their entrepreneurial spirit and ability to innovate even as they've grown and their industries have changed.

The Findings

Both companies encourage employees at all levels to take on leadership roles. They also let the actions of employees collectively determine which growth projects to fund. As a result, key decisions are aligned with strategic goals—and bureaucracy is kept to a minimum.

Entrepreneurial Leaders

Much more is expected of frontline leaders at PARC and Gore than of similar employees in more-bureaucratic settings. Entrepreneurial leaders "sense and seize" growth opportunities, lobby for early-stage resources, pull colleagues in with their vision for moving forward, and fully exploit the opportunities that pan out. Most of those we observed exhibited three qualities.

Self-confidence and a willingness to act

These leaders believe in themselves. They experiment, and they're resilient in the face of failure. An engineer at Gore, for example, became interested in a better way to seal fleecy material using the company's proprietary waterproof-membrane technology—something that had baffled specialists. He got hold of some sheep-shearing tools and spent months in his spare time trying various methods to shave fleece, until he finally arrived at a solution. He and colleagues then found a machine that could duplicate the method but do the job faster and better. At that point the project would normally have gone to a different team for development, but the engineer advocated to stay with it in a leadership role, believing he grasped the potential for exploitation better than anyone else could.

A strategic mindset

Entrepreneurial leaders understand the goals of their organization, business unit, and team at a very deep level. When they take action, they do so to advance those goals.

Often that deep understanding exists because the organization has formulated and communicated simple rules of operation. An engineer at Gore told us, "It's got to be novel, and we make sure the product does what it says it does. And we need to make sure that the revenue will be big enough—a $500,000 opportunity isn't going to get a lot of effort out of us." Even low-level technicians at PARC can talk with sophistication about its business model: the markets the company wants to serve, the percentage split between commercial and government contracts, the expected financial returns, and the available resources.

Entrepreneurial leaders build on this high-level understanding of corporate goals with regular ground-level exposure to customers' needs. Through external outreach they sense new opportunities and refine product ideas. One told us, "We have a lot of people who explore the changing needs of real users . . . . here are the trends, here is where things are shifting."

Many of these leaders have so fully absorbed their organization's strategic goals that they are adept at deciding which investments of time meet multiple goals. A senior leader at PARC told us his people aim for "triple word scores" (a phrase borrowed from Scrabble): opportunities that contribute to success on at least three strategic fronts. One team, he said, aimed to "publish, get government funding, produce commercial outcomes, and create synergies with the rest of the organization"—all from one initiative.

Absorbing cultural norms—"how we do things here"—is as much a part of developing a strategic mindset as is understanding the business model. At Gore the expectation is that every innovation will build on the company's core materials technology, and business dealings must be fair to all stakeholders. At PARC "good taste" is a mantra, and technologies are expected to be best-in-class.

The Downsides of Nimble Leadership

THIS SYSTEM OF MANAGEMENT is a powerful driver of innovation and reinvention, but it isn't for the faint of heart, for several reasons:

It's really complicated.
These organizations have lots of moving parts. That many of those parts are self-managing doesn't make coordinating them any easier; in some ways it makes coordination harder. And leaders have to believe the system will work; otherwise it's tempting to hang on to bureaucratic controls.

Change at these companies (ironically) can be hard to pull off.
Because people at PARC and Gore are used to consultative, crowdsourced decision making, they sometimes balk at changes they perceive as having been imposed on them. Other times they might be frustrated with the slow pace of change.

The system doesn't suit everyone.
Even some very talented people aren't comfortable with the degree of autonomy these organizations allow; they'd rather be given clear direction and specific goals. (Both PARC and Gore spend a great deal of time during the hiring process exploring cultural fit.)

Even if it is a good match for someone, learning it takes time.
Employees at PARC and Gore go through a lengthy and expensive socialization process.

An ability to attract others
Leaders at PARC and Gore aren't handed followers; they must earn them. Many new product-development projects aren't started at the behest of a high-level manager; they happen because an individual or a group gets interested in an opportunity, does some digging, and figures out whether it's worth further investment. At that point the initiators must be able to pull people (and financial resources) onto a team. That takes persuasiveness, confidence, and (often) a good product-innovation track record.

Once volunteers have formed a team, the entrepreneurial leader initially takes the reins—but that doesn't mean people follow blindly. Both firms we studied are committed to collective decision making.

This was instilled at PARC in its early days. The first head of its computer lab, for instance, famously "never made technical decisions; the group as a whole did." A manager at Gore said, "People in this culture will often push back and say, 'I don't agree with that, and here's why I think it won't work.'" A good team leader, he added, might respond, "OK, that's interesting, and it's new information." So entrepreneurial leaders need to be confident enough to pull people in but open to changing course if presented with an evidence-based argument. (On some teams decisions require a consensus; on others the leader makes the call once the pros and cons have been discussed.) People join and leave teams in a somewhat organic fashion dictated by the project's needs and their own interests.

Taken together, these qualities—self-confidence, a strategic mindset, and the ability to attract others—allow new product-development ideas that are aligned with strategic goals to emerge and grow in a free-flowing, bottom-up fashion. And those qualities thrive in part because of three long-standing cultural touchstones. The first is *job autonomy.* Gore and to a lesser extent PARC were created with the idea that employees would have significant choice in their work assignments and teams. The freedom to shift work commitments enables the rapid, voluntary redeployment of people to new projects as needs arise.

The second touchstone is *the practice of making many small bets and providing just-in-time resources.* It's impossible to know which ideas will work out, so many bets are needed. At both organizations a collective review process is in place to determine which ideas will move forward, ensuring that the best ones are chosen and that funds are provided without a long wait for senior team approval. The third touchstone is *stepping-up and stepping-down leadership.* Both companies embrace the idea that everyone, not just those in formal positions of power, can lead. A manager at Gore told us that all new product development participants need "a willingness to know when they should be leading"—which implies also being able to discern when they should be following. The process demands humility, respect, and putting the success of the team and the company above one's own achievements.

Enabling Leaders

Leaders who have more experience than their entrepreneurial col-leagues (and are often above them in the flattened hierarchy) focus on helping project leaders develop as individuals, navigate organi-zational hurdles, connect with others, and stay in touch with larger business shifts. Certain skills are key.

Coaching and development

Enabling leaders often act more like coaches or mentors than a tradi-tional boss would (and they might not be the formal manager of the person they are coaching). They tend to ask questions rather than offer explicit direction. One sales manager described his relationship with a coach this way: "He was a manufacturing guy. He didn't know anything about sales, but somehow—in half an hour I'd come away with a sense of 'now I get it' . . . . He'd get me to the right questions. It was never 'I think you should go left' but 'Do you think you should go right or left?'" The enabling leaders we spoke with had learned not to jump in to solve problems for entrepreneurial leaders. One told us, "The temptation is to say, 'OK, I'll fix it; I'll call that person for you.' But when you do that, you're enabling dependence."

A key part of coaching is helping teams navigate the product development process—and in that context, an enabling leader may become a more active problem solver. (Often these leaders have started out on project teams and have a deep understanding of the issues that can arise.) When a team at Gore needed to get colleagues excited about a project, an enabling leader helped members think through how to position the opportunity. He got them onto the agenda of a divisional team leadership meeting and coached them on their presentation, the questions to anticipate, and what angle was most likely to galvanize the group.

These leaders also help people think about their own develop-ment, matching the needs of the business with employees' needs for increasingly complex roles. This can be a fairly straightforward task, owing to the nature of self-organizing teams: If someone has attracted followers and done a bang-up job on a challenging project, he or she will be sought-after for new initiatives and broader tasks. For other workers, enabling leaders offer feedback on how to improve.

Connecting

While coaching supports entrepreneurial leaders in their individual growth, connecting helps them experience "creative collisions." Enabling leaders typically have a broader view than do team leaders of what's happening around and outside the organization, so they can see opportunities to create value and can spot "structural holes" that need to be filled. In some cases they connect entrepreneurs to end users; in others they provide connections to similar or complementary projects within the firm. They also ensure that various functional groups—marketing, sales, and regulatory specialists, for example—know what the other functions are up to. Connectors tend to travel to broaden their already-wide networks and link people across functional and geographic borders. One manager described a superconnector in the product development space. "We have one guy seeing all the product concepts . . . and he's constantly gauging them all," he told us. "He can say, 'There's a guy in Arizona, one in Tapania, and one in France, all thinking the same way. . . . Let's have them all sit in a room and work together."

Communicating

We noted above that even lower-level people at PARC and Gore have a sophisticated understanding of their firm's business model. Enabling leaders put a great deal of energy into keeping that understanding up-to-date by sharing information about emerging opportunities and changes in the external environment.

The simplest form this communication takes is making sure one part of the organization knows what the other parts are doing (and that it all adds up to something coherent). That's especially important—and challenging—when regional priorities don't perfectly align with global goals. One enabling leader told us, "Twice a year we meet with the divisions and say, 'Here's what we'll do, here's how you'll benefit, here are the projects we're working on for you.

Are we missing something? What are your business problems? We're you, and you're us.'"

Enabling leaders also keep an eye on maintaining the organization's values in new business contexts. This works best when they fold communication into a business conversation rather than present it as a blanket directive. One project leader at Gore said that a manager reviewing a royalty agreement under development with a supplier immediately wanted to know, "Is it fair to them?" That simple question reinforced one of Gore's core values: that the company won't prosper over the long term if its partners don't.

Two additional cultural touchstones support enabling leaders' work. First, PARC and Gore have traditionally valued *rapid access to information and high levels of connectivity* throughout their firms. Gore tries to keep plant size to a human-community scale of fewer than 300 people to maximize face-to-face interaction and information exchange. With changes in technology and the rise of global teams, new IT and communication tools also foster interaction. The firm asks most employees to spend much of their first six months building networks across the organization. And PARC was the first company in the world in which all employees were electronically connected.

Second, both firms use *vision, values, and simple rules as decision guardrails,* as the Gore manager's concern about fairness to suppliers illustrates. We've noticed that often these decision guardrails support growth, innovation, and cultural values—and we've been fascinated to see that they also provide a mechanism for managing risk. Everyone at Gore knows the "Don't poke holes below the waterline" principle: If something makes them uncomfortable, employees have an obligation to stop the conversation and say, "I think this is a risk for the company"—and the group then consults with knowledge experts about the issue. (If you damage a ship below the waterline, it sinks.)

Architecting Leaders

Senior leaders focus most of their attention on big-picture issues that require changes in organizational culture, structure, and resources.

How Satya Nadella Is Reinventing Microsoft's Culture

WHEN 22-YEAR VETERAN SATYA NADELLA became CEO of Microsoft, in 2014, the company needed a serious reboot. The stock price had stalled, product development was lagging, and employees were more focused on competing than collaborating. This was not what one would call a nimble organization. The firm needed to get out of mobile phone telephony and invest heavily in cloud computing—but for that to succeed, the culture would have to be rebuilt from the ground up. Nadella's efforts to that end bear many hallmarks of the organizational form we studied at PARC and Gore, echoing the cultural touchstones, coaching style of leadership, and continuous learning we observed at those organizations. (Herminia Ibarra, Aneeta Rattan, and Anna Johnston described Microsoft's cultural changes in a recent London Business School case study.)

Nadella used a single overarching metaphor to guide those changes: Carol Dweck's concept that a growth mindset, rather than a fixed one, is key to developing a dynamic, learning-focused culture. (He told a *Wall Street Journal* reporter that his wife "forced" him to read Dweck's *Mindset: The New Psychology of Success*.) With help from a "culture cabinet," he announced the pillars of the new strategic direction: customer obsession, diversity and inclusion, and the idea, captured in the phrase "one Microsoft," that everyone needed to pull in the same direction.

Nadella introduced multiple changes to how decisions were made, performance was evaluated, and leaders were expected to behave. First he built a new senior team—one he could trust to both raise tough questions and function cohesively once a decision was reached. He chose members for technical competence, of course, but was just as interested in whether they were empathetic and respectful to employees at all levels. He wanted to change

Sometimes the game board needs to change because of shifts in ownership or governance structure. In a 2002 Xerox restructuring, for instance, PARC (which had been a division of Xerox) became a stand-alone subsidiary and consequently needed to diversify the types of businesses it was in. Survival required new commercial clients, more government work, and the seeding of start-ups, and the message went out from on high. At other times the game board needs to change because of shifts in the external environment for which internal groups are unprepared. None of Gore's subunits had

how company leaders conversed with and guided people. His predecessors, Bill Gates and Steve Ballmer, had engaged in "precision questioning"—the sometimes-aggressive dismantling of other people's arguments, which conveyed impatience with imperfection and could create an atmosphere of outright hostility. Nadella, who says he learned empathy as the parent of a special-needs child, wanted to convey curiosity instead and proceeded on the assumption that he could learn from whoever was speaking. He expected other leaders to do the same.

Stacked rankings, which required that 10% of employees receive a "poor" performance rating, had pretty much killed collaboration at the company, Nadella thought. He substituted continuous coaching and gave local managers more control over compensation.

He also urged leaders to model growth-mindset behaviors—which means admitting when they make mistakes. He has played role-model-in-chief in this regard, too. During a conference on women in computing, he advised a questioner to be patient and have "faith that the system will actually give you the right raises." Not surprisingly, women did not find this advice helpful, and they made their objections very clear. Rather than stand his ground or wait for the noise to die down, Nadella told employees he'd given a completely wrong answer and learned a valuable lesson.

Changing Microsoft's culture hasn't been easy, and the process isn't complete. But the company's performance since 2014 has been extraordinary—and senior leaders believe that changing the culture was the key to changing the company's fortunes.

a broad enough view to see the value of having manufacturing facilities in Asia, but the top team determined that they would be in the company's best interests and redirected resources accordingly.

Architecting leaders not only respond to external threats and opportunities but also serve as caretakers of internal operations. As such they might amplify a move that originated from below, as when Gore's leadership expanded on a push toward greater sustainability that had been championed by enabling and entrepreneurial leaders. They might fill holes no local unit had perceived. They might find ways to make the company more effective or efficient, as when senior leaders at PARC initiated a drive to hire PhDs who were great scientists with entrepreneurial interests.

Senior leaders at Gore were worried about declining success rates for new product development efforts, so they introduced the "real/win/worth" process to help entrepreneurial leaders, in consultation with functional leaders, decide whether to pursue opportunities. This involved three simple but profound questions:

- Are the product and the market real?

- Can the product and the company win in the market?

- Is the investment worth it, and does it make strategic sense?

Finally, changes might be called for because individual groups are making decisions that are sensible locally but are suboptimal for the company as a whole. For example, groups are often interested in developing their own computer, HR, and financial systems—but experience shows that decentralizing those functions hinders coordination and collaboration across the firm.

If big changes are in order, senior managers may need to make top-down decisions, which of course flies in the face of collective decision making. When that happens, leaders need to spend time explaining—and listening. Even so, some employees will resist the change, while others wish senior leaders would just "rip the Band-Aid off" and move decisively ahead. Facing such inflection points, architectural leaders probably won't succeed unless they have an excellent personal reputation within the firm—and the company has an equally good reputation with external stakeholders. (See the sidebar "How Satya Nadella Is Reinventing Microsoft's Culture" for a description of one company's drive to institute change and become nimbler.)

A Whole Greater Than the Sum of Its Parts

The cultural touchstones we've discussed support all three types of leadership, and together they create a system that's adaptive and self-reinforcing. Because employees have so much autonomy, talented people are always available to start and join new projects. Because power is distributed throughout the organization, people are free to push forward good project ideas. Because people get early leadership training and build strong networks, they learn to engage the right people. The creative collisions facilitated by connecting far-flung people and communicating shared goals transform siloed projects into synergistic collaborations. The collective allocation of resources on an as-needed basis means that promising projects get the support they need. And the emphasis on explicit, widely shared values and simple rules ensures that investment decisions are aligned with organizational priorities.

Three aspects of the system are worth highlighting.

Distributed leadership

At both PARC and Gore a remarkable number of employees refer to themselves as leaders; the culture expects them to. As a result, the companies have a cadre of ready-to-go leaders, and the reins really do pass from one set of hands to another easily, as the situation requires.

The different types of leaders interact with one another all the time, of course, and their tasks are certainly not 100% distinct. (We could have included sections on "strategic mindset" and "communication" under any of the types, for instance.) We don't believe one person can fill all three leadership functions simultaneously, but the roles are more fluid than we've made them sound. A natural-born enabling leader will connect, communicate, and coach, whatever his title or hierarchical position, just as a brilliant entrepreneurial leader will keep coming up with new product ideas while she's running the company. We saw several enabling leaders initiate and manage large-scale change campaigns that might more predictably have been handled by architecting leaders.

The power of the many

Academics use the word "emergence" to describe a process whereby order at the system level arises from individual interactions at lower levels of aggregation. We saw that play out at PARC and Gore. As we described above, the volunteers who show up for a new product development team (or don't) are a big factor in whether the project is funded—and if more people vote "yes" by joining the team later on, resources continue to flow in. Time will tell whether this form of crowdsourced strategy combined with architecting leadership works better than decisions handed down by the CEO, but the track record so far is good. And with many people reading the environment, talking with customers, and acting on what they see, the whole organization is nimble and able to move in new directions.

Processes that balance freedom and control

When we speak with leaders about this kind of system, most agree intellectually that power, decision making, and resource allocation should be distributed. But making that happen is another matter. Their great fear is that the organization will fall into chaos. But PARC and Gore show that it's possible to build processes that, taken together, can maintain order better than any bureaucratic regulations while also supporting innovation. We've described those processes throughout this article, but let's look explicitly at some of the ways in which they help maintain order.

- Because individuals need to be persuaded to join a project, their feedback and misgivings are incorporated early in the development process, and talent is drained away from less-promising projects.

- Because enabling leaders devote much time and energy to discussions about new information, nobody's strategic mindset becomes inflexible.

- Because cultural values and simple rules relating to the business model are part of everyday conversations and decision processes, people don't go off in myriad directions.

- The collective vetting ensures that investment decisions aren't determined by a leader's pet projects.

- Because projects begin with small bets and are reinvested in iteratively, one bad bet won't bring down the entire operation.

The leadership roles, cultural norms, and system-level checks we've described give these organizations a leg up with employees that's difficult to define but quite tangible nonetheless. On each visit to Gore we heard about some new, usually unexpected area of interest—and recent explorations have included everything from insulated cables that enable reliable Wi-Fi on airplanes to footwear technology that provides warmth without bulk. Remarkable energy and joie de vivre pervade both PARC and Gore. Companies that need to improve their new-product hit rate—and boost employee engagement—should take note.

Originally published in July–August 2019. Reprint R1904D

Note

(Disclosure: W.L. Gore covered some research costs for this project under a legal agreement protecting the researchers' independence.)

The Focused Leader

by Daniel Goleman

A PRIMARY TASK OF LEADERSHIP is to direct attention. To do so, leaders must learn to focus their own attention. When we speak about being focused, we commonly mean thinking about one thing while filtering out distractions. But a wealth of recent research in neuroscience shows that we focus in many ways, for different purposes, drawing on different neural pathways—some of which work in concert, while others tend to stand in opposition.

Grouping these modes of attention into three broad buckets—focusing on *yourself,* focusing on *others,* and focusing on *the wider world*—sheds new light on the practice of many essential leadership skills. Focusing inward and focusing constructively on others helps leaders cultivate the primary elements of emotional intelligence. A fuller understanding of how they focus on the wider world can improve their ability to devise strategy, innovate, and manage organizations.

Every leader needs to cultivate this triad of awareness, in abundance and in the proper balance, because a failure to focus inward leaves you rudderless, a failure to focus on others renders you clueless, and a failure to focus outward may leave you blindsided.

Focusing on Yourself

Emotional intelligence begins with self-awareness—getting in touch with your inner voice. Leaders who heed their inner voices can draw on more resources to make better decisions and connect with their authentic selves. But what does that entail? A look at how people focus inward can make this abstract concept more concrete.

Self-awareness

Hearing your inner voice is a matter of paying careful attention to internal physiological signals. These subtle cues are monitored by the insula, which is tucked behind the frontal lobes of the brain. Attention given to any part of the body amps up the insula's sensitivity to that part. Tune in to your heartbeat, and the insula activates more neurons in that circuitry. How well people can sense their heartbeats has, in fact, become a standard way to measure their self-awareness.

Gut feelings are messages from the insula and the amygdala, which the neuroscientist Antonio Damasio, of the University of Southern California, calls *somatic markers*. Those messages are sensations that something "feels" right or wrong. Somatic markers simplify decision making by guiding our attention toward better options. They're hardly foolproof (how often was that feeling that you left the stove on correct?), so the more comprehensively we read them, the better we use our intuition. (See "Are You Skimming This Sidebar?")

Consider, for example, the implications of an analysis of interviews conducted by a group of British researchers with 118 professional traders and 10 senior managers at four City of London investment banks. The most successful traders (whose annual income averaged £500,000) were neither the ones who relied entirely on analytics nor the ones who just went with their guts. They focused on a full range of emotions, which they used to judge the value of their intuition. When they suffered losses, they acknowledged their anxiety, became more cautious, and took fewer risks. The least successful traders (whose income averaged only £100,000) tended to ignore their anxiety and keep going with their guts. Because they failed to heed a wider array of internal signals, they were misled.

Zeroing in on sensory impressions of ourselves in the moment is one major element of self-awareness. But another is critical to leadership: combining our experiences across time into a coherent view of our authentic selves.

Idea in Brief

The Problem

A primary task of leadership is to direct attention. To do so, leaders must learn to focus their own attention.

The Argument

People commonly think of "being focused" as filtering out distractions while concentrating on one thing. But a wealth of recent neuroscience research shows that we focus attention in many ways, for different purposes, while drawing on different neural pathways.

The Solution

Every leader needs to cultivate a triad of awareness—an inward focus, a focus on others, and an outward focus. Focusing inward and focusing on others helps leaders cultivate emotional intelligence. Focusing outward can improve their ability to devise strategy, innovate, and manage organizations.

To be authentic is to be the same person to others as you are to yourself. In part that entails paying attention to what others think of you, particularly people whose opinions you esteem and who will be candid in their feedback. A variety of focus that is useful here is *open awareness,* in which we broadly notice what's going on around us without getting caught up in or swept away by any particular thing. In this mode we don't judge, censor, or tune out; we simply perceive.

Leaders who are more accustomed to giving input than to receiving it may find this tricky. Someone who has trouble sustaining open awareness typically gets snagged by irritating details, such as fellow travelers in the airport security line who take forever getting their carry-ons into the scanner. Someone who can keep her attention in open mode will notice the travelers but not worry about them, and will take in more of her surroundings. (See the sidebar "Expand Your Awareness.")

Of course, being open to input doesn't guarantee that someone will provide it. Sadly, life affords us few chances to learn how others really see us, and even fewer for executives as they rise through the ranks. That may be why one of the most popular and overenrolled courses at Harvard Business School is Bill George's Authentic Leadership Development, in which George has created what he calls True North groups to heighten this aspect of self-awareness.

Are You Skimming This Sidebar?

DO YOU HAVE TROUBLE remembering what someone has just told you in conversation? Did you drive to work this morning on autopilot? Do you focus more on your smartphone than on the person you're having lunch with?

Attention is a mental muscle; like any other muscle, it can be strengthened through the right kind of exercise. The fundamental rep for building deliberate attention is simple: When your mind wanders, notice that it has wandered, bring it back to your desired point of focus, and keep it there as long as you can. That basic exercise is at the root of virtually every kind of meditation. Meditation builds concentration and calmness and facilitates recovery from the agitation of stress.

So does a video game called Tenacity, now in development by a design group and neuroscientists at the University of Wisconsin. Slated for release in 2014, the game offers a leisurely journey through any of half a dozen scenes, from a barren desert to a fantasy staircase spiraling heavenward. At the beginner's level you tap an iPad screen with one finger every time you exhale; the challenge is to tap two fingers with every fifth breath. As you move to higher levels, you're presented with more distractions—a helicopter flies into view, a plane does a flip, a flock of birds suddenly scud by.

When players are attuned to the rhythm of their breathing, they experience the strengthening of selective attention as a feeling of calm focus, as in meditation. Stanford University is exploring that connection at its Calming Technology Lab, which is developing relaxing devices, such as a belt that detects your breathing rate. Should a chock-full in-box, for instance, trigger what has been called e-mail apnea, an iPhone app can guide you through exercises to calm your breathing and your mind.

These groups (which anyone can form) are based on the precept that self-knowledge begins with self-revelation. Accordingly, they are open and intimate, "a safe place," George explains, "where members can discuss personal issues they do not feel they can raise elsewhere—often not even with their closest family members." What good does that do? "We don't know who we are until we hear ourselves speaking the story of our lives to those we trust," George says. It's a structured way to match our view of our true selves with the views our most trusted colleagues have—an external check on our authenticity.

Expand Your Awareness

JUST AS A CAMERA LENS can be set narrowly on a single point or more widely to take in a panoramic view, you can focus tightly or expansively.

One measure of open awareness presents people with a stream of letters and numbers, such as S, K, O, E, 4, R, T, 2, H, P. In scanning the stream, many people will notice the first number, 4, but after that their attention blinks. Those firmly in open awareness mode will register the second number as well.

Strengthening the ability to maintain open awareness requires leaders to do something that verges on the unnatural: cultivate at least sometimes a willingness to not be in control, not offer up their own views, not judge others. That's less a matter of deliberate action than of attitude adjustment.

One path to making that adjustment is through the classic power of positive thinking, because pessimism narrows our focus, whereas positive emotions widen our attention and our receptiveness to the new and unexpected. A simple way to shift into positive mode is to ask yourself, "If everything worked out perfectly in my life, what would I be doing in 10 years?" Why is that effective? Because when you're in an upbeat mood, the University of Wisconsin neuroscientist Richard Davidson has found, your brain's left prefrontal area lights up. That area harbors the circuitry that reminds us how great we'll feel when we reach some long-sought goal.

"Talking about positive goals and dreams activates brain centers that open you up to new possibilities," says Richard Boyatzis, a psychologist at Case Western Reserve. "But if you change the conversation to what you should do to fix yourself, it closes you down. . . . You need the negative to survive, but the positive to thrive."

Self-control

"Cognitive control" is the scientific term for putting one's attention where one wants it and keeping it there in the face of temptation to wander. This focus is one aspect of the brain's executive function, which is located in the prefrontal cortex. A colloquial term for it is "willpower."

Cognitive control enables executives to pursue a goal despite distractions and setbacks. The same neural circuitry that allows such a single-minded pursuit of goals also manages unruly emotions. Good cognitive control can be seen in people who stay calm in a crisis, tame their own agitation, and recover from a debacle or defeat.

Decades' worth of research demonstrates the singular importance of willpower to leadership success. Particularly compelling is a longitudinal study tracking the fates of all 1,037 children born during a single year in the 1970s in the New Zealand city of Dunedin. For several years during childhood the children were given a battery of tests of willpower, including the psychologist Walter Mischel's legendary "marshmallow test"—a choice between eating one marshmallow right away and getting two by waiting 15 minutes. In Mischel's experiments, roughly a third of children grab the marshmallow on the spot, another third hold out for a while longer, and a third manage to make it through the entire quarter hour.

Years later, when the children in the Dunedin study were in their 30s and all but 4% of them had been tracked down again, the researchers found that those who'd had the cognitive control to resist the marshmallow longest were significantly healthier, more successful financially, and more law-abiding than the ones who'd been unable to hold out at all. In fact, statistical analysis showed that a child's level of self-control was a more powerful predictor of financial success than IQ, social class, or family circumstance.

How we focus holds the key to exercising willpower, Mischel says. Three subvarieties of cognitive control are at play when you pit self-restraint against self-gratification: the ability to voluntarily disengage your focus from an object of desire; the ability to resist distraction so that you don't gravitate back to that object; and the ability to concentrate on the future goal and imagine how good you will feel when you achieve it. As adults the children of Dunedin may have been held hostage to their younger selves, but they need not have been, because the power to focus can be developed. (See the sidebar "Learning Self-Restraint.")

Focusing on Others

The word "attention" comes from the Latin *attendere,* meaning "to reach toward." This is a perfect definition of focus on others, which is the foundation of empathy and of an ability to build social relationships—the second and third pillars of emotional intelligence.

Learning Self-Restraint

QUICK, NOW. HERE'S A TEST of cognitive control. In what direction is the middle arrow in each row pointing?

→ → → ← ←
→ ← ← ← ←
→ → ← → →

The test, called the Eriksen Flanker Task, gauges your susceptibility to distraction. When it's taken under laboratory conditions, differences of a thousandth of a second can be detected in the speed with which subjects perceive which direction the middle arrows are pointing. The stronger their cognitive control, the less susceptible they are to distraction.

Interventions to strengthen cognitive control can be as unsophisticated as a game of Simon Says or Red Light—any exercise in which you are asked to stop on cue. Research suggests that the better a child gets at playing Musical Chairs, the stronger his or her prefrontal wiring for cognitive control will become.

Operating on a similarly simple principle is a social and emotional learning (SEL) method that's used to strengthen cognitive control in schoolchildren across the United States. When confronted by an upsetting problem, the children are told to think of a traffic signal. The red light means stop, calm down, and think before you act. The yellow light means slow down and think of several possible solutions. The green light means try out a plan and see how it works. Thinking in these terms allows the children to shift away from amygdala-driven impulses to prefrontal-driven deliberate behavior.

It's never too late for adults to strengthen these circuits as well. Daily sessions of mindfulness practice work in a way similar to Musical Chairs and SEL. In these sessions you focus your attention on your breathing and practice tracking your thoughts and feelings without getting swept away by them. Whenever you notice that your mind has wandered, you simply return it to your breath. It sounds easy—but try it for 10 minutes, and you'll find there's a learning curve.

Executives who can effectively focus on others are easy to recognize. They are the ones who find common ground, whose opinions carry the most weight, and with whom other people want to work. They emerge as natural leaders regardless of organizational or social rank.

The empathy triad

We talk about empathy most commonly as a single attribute. But a close look at where leaders are focusing when they exhibit it reveals three distinct kinds, each important for leadership effectiveness:

- *cognitive empathy*—the ability to understand another person's perspective;
- *emotional empathy*—the ability to feel what someone else feels;
- *empathic concern*—the ability to sense what another person needs from you.

Cognitive empathy enables leaders to explain themselves in meaningful ways—a skill essential to getting the best performance from their direct reports. Contrary to what you might expect, exercising cognitive empathy requires leaders to think about feelings rather than to feel them directly.

An inquisitive nature feeds cognitive empathy. As one successful executive with this trait puts it, "I've always just wanted to learn everything, to understand anybody that I was around—why they thought what they did, why they did what they did, what worked for them, and what didn't work." But cognitive empathy is also an outgrowth of self-awareness. The executive circuits that allow us to think about our own thoughts and to monitor the feelings that flow from them let us apply the same reasoning to other people's minds when we choose to direct our attention that way.

Emotional empathy is important for effective mentoring, managing clients, and reading group dynamics. It springs from ancient parts of the brain beneath the cortex—the amygdala, the hypothalamus, the hippocampus, and the orbitofrontal cortex—that allow us to feel fast without thinking deeply. They tune us in by arousing in our bodies the emotional states of others: I literally feel your pain. My brain patterns match up with yours when I listen to you tell a gripping story. As Tania Singer, the director of the social neuroscience department at the Max Planck Institute for Human Cognitive and Brain Sciences, in Leipzig, says, "You need to understand your own feelings to understand the feelings of others." Accessing your capacity for emotional empathy depends on combining two kinds of attention: a deliberate focus on your own echoes of someone else's

When Empathy Needs to Be Learned

EMOTIONAL EMPATHY CAN BE DEVELOPED. That's the conclusion suggested by research conducted with physicians by Helen Riess, the director of the Empathy and Relational Science Program at Boston's Massachusetts General Hospital. To help the physicians monitor themselves, she set up a program in which they learned to focus using deep, diaphragmatic breathing and to cultivate a certain detachment—to watch an interaction from the ceiling, as it were, rather than being lost in their own thoughts and feelings. "Suspending your own involvement to observe what's going on gives you a mindful awareness of the interaction without being completely reactive," says Riess. "You can see if your own physiology is charged up or balanced. You can notice what's transpiring in the situation." If a doctor realizes that she's feeling irritated, for instance, that may be a signal that the patient is bothered too.

Those who are utterly at a loss may be able to prime emotional empathy essentially by faking it until they make it, Riess adds. If you act in a caring way—looking people in the eye and paying attention to their expressions, even when you don't particularly want to—you may start to feel more engaged.

feelings and an open awareness of that person's face, voice, and other external signs of emotion. (See the sidebar "When Empathy Needs to Be Learned.")

Empathic concern, which is closely related to emotional empathy, enables you to sense not just how people feel but what they need from you. It's what you want in your doctor, your spouse—and your boss. Empathic concern has its roots in the circuitry that compels parents' attention to their children. Watch where people's eyes go when someone brings an adorable baby into a room, and you'll see this mammalian brain center leaping into action.

One neural theory holds that the response is triggered in the amygdala by the brain's radar for sensing danger and in the prefrontal cortex by the release of oxytocin, the chemical for caring. This implies that empathic concern is a double-edged feeling. We intuitively experience the distress of another as our own. But in deciding whether we will meet that person's needs, we deliberately weigh how much we value his or her well-being.

Getting this intuition-deliberation mix right has great implications. Those whose sympathetic feelings become too strong may themselves suffer. In the helping professions, this can lead to

When Empathy Needs to Be Controlled

GETTING A GRIP on our impulse to empathize with other people's feelings can help us make better decisions when someone's emotional flood threatens to overwhelm us.

Ordinarily, when we see someone pricked with a pin, our brains emit a signal indicating that our own pain centers are echoing that distress. But physicians learn in medical school to block even such automatic responses. Their attentional anesthetic seems to be deployed by the temporal-parietal junction and regions of the prefrontal cortex, a circuit that boosts concentration by tuning out emotions. That's what is happening in your brain when you distance yourself from others in order to stay calm and help them. The same neural network kicks in when we see a problem in an emotionally overheated environment and need to focus on looking for a solution. If you're talking with someone who is upset, this system helps you understand the person's perspective intellectually by shifting from the heart-to-heart of emotional empathy to the head-to-heart of cognitive empathy.

---

compassion fatigue; in executives, it can create distracting feelings of anxiety about people and circumstances that are beyond anyone's control. But those who protect themselves by deadening their feelings may lose touch with empathy. Empathic concern requires us to manage our personal distress without numbing ourselves to the pain of others. (See the sidebar "When Empathy Needs to Be Controlled.")

What's more, some lab research suggests that the appropriate application of empathic concern is critical to making moral judgments. Brain scans have revealed that when volunteers listened to tales of people subjected to physical pain, their own brain centers for experiencing such pain lit up instantly. But if the story was about psychological suffering, the higher brain centers involved in empathic concern and compassion took longer to activate. Some time is needed to grasp the psychological and moral dimensions of a situation. The more distracted we are, the less we can cultivate the subtler forms of empathy and compassion.

Building relationships

People who lack social sensitivity are easy to spot—at least for other people. They are the clueless among us. The CFO who is technically competent but bullies some people, freezes out others, and plays favorites—but when you point out what he has just done, shifts the blame, gets angry, or thinks that you're the problem—is not trying to be a jerk; he's utterly unaware of his shortcomings.

Social sensitivity appears to be related to cognitive empathy. Cognitively empathic executives do better at overseas assignments, for instance, presumably because they quickly pick up implicit norms and learn the unique mental models of a new culture. Attention to social context lets us act with skill no matter what the situation, instinctively follow the universal algorithm for etiquette, and behave in ways that put others at ease. (In another age this might have been called good manners.)

Circuitry that converges on the anterior hippocampus reads social context and leads us intuitively to act differently with, say, our college buddies than with our families or our colleagues. In concert with the deliberative prefrontal cortex, it squelches the impulse to do something inappropriate. Accordingly, one brain test for sensitivity to context assesses the function of the hippocampus. The University of Wisconsin neuroscientist Richard Davidson hypothesizes that people who are most alert to social situations exhibit stronger activity and more connections between the hippocampus and the prefrontal cortex than those who just can't seem to get it right.

The same circuits may be at play when we map social networks in a group—a skill that lets us navigate the relationships in those networks well. People who excel at organizational influence can not only sense the flow of personal connections but also name the people whose opinions hold most sway, and so focus on persuading those who will persuade others.

Alarmingly, research suggests that as people rise through the ranks and gain power, their ability to perceive and maintain personal connections tends to suffer a sort of psychic attrition. In studying encounters between people of varying status, Dacher Keltner, a psychologist at Berkeley, has found that higher-ranking individuals consistently focus their gaze less on lower-ranking people and are more likely to interrupt or to monopolize the conversation.

In fact, mapping attention to power in an organization gives a clear indication of hierarchy: The longer it takes Person A to respond to Person B, the more relative power Person A has. Map response times across an entire organization, and you'll get a remarkably accurate chart of social standing. The boss leaves e-mails unanswered for hours; those lower down respond within minutes. This is so predictable that an algorithm for it—called automated social hierarchy detection—has been developed at Columbia University. Intelligence agencies reportedly are applying the algorithm to suspected terrorist gangs to piece together chains of influence and identify central figures.

But the real point is this: Where we see ourselves on the social ladder sets the default for how much attention we pay. This should be a warning to top executives, who need to respond to fast-moving competitive situations by tapping the full range of ideas and talents within an organization. Without a deliberate shift in attention, their natural inclination may be to ignore smart ideas from the lower ranks.

Focusing on the Wider World

Leaders with a strong outward focus are not only good listeners but also good questioners. They are visionaries who can sense the far-flung consequences of local decisions and imagine how the choices they make today will play out in the future. They are open to the surprising ways in which seemingly unrelated data can inform their central interests. Melinda Gates offered up a cogent example when she remarked on 60 Minutes that her husband was the kind of person who would read an entire book about fertilizer. Charlie Rose asked, Why fertilizer? The connection was obvious to Bill Gates, who is constantly looking for technological advances that can save lives on a massive scale. "A few billion people would have to die if we hadn't come up with fertilizer," he replied.

Focusing on strategy

Any business school course on strategy will give you the two main elements: exploitation of your current advantage and exploration for new ones. Brain scans that were performed on 63 seasoned business decision makers as they pursued or switched between exploitative and exploratory strategies revealed the specific circuits involved. Not surprisingly, exploitation requires concentration on the job at hand, whereas exploration demands open awareness to recognize new possibilities. But exploitation is accompanied by activity in the brain's circuitry for anticipation and reward. In other words, it feels good to coast along in a familiar routine. When we switch to exploration, we have to make a deliberate cognitive effort to disengage from that routine in order to roam widely and pursue fresh paths.

What keeps us from making that effort? Sleep deprivation, drinking, stress, and mental overload all interfere with the executive circuitry used to make the cognitive switch. To sustain the outward focus that leads to innovation, we need some uninterrupted time in which to reflect and refresh our focus.

The wellsprings of innovation

In an era when almost everyone has access to the same information, new value arises from putting ideas together in novel ways and asking smart questions that open up untapped potential. Moments before we have a creative insight, the brain shows a third-of-a-second spike in gamma waves, indicating the synchrony of far-flung brain cells. The more neurons firing in sync, the bigger the spike. Its timing suggests that what's happening is the formation of a new neural network—presumably creating a fresh association.

But it would be making too much of this to see gamma waves as a secret to creativity. A classic model of creativity suggests how the various modes of attention play key roles. First we prepare our minds by gathering a wide variety of pertinent information, and then we alternate between concentrating intently on the problem and letting our minds wander freely. Those activities translate roughly into vigilance, when while immersing ourselves in all kinds of input, we remain alert for anything relevant to the problem at hand; selective attention to the specific creative challenge; and open awareness, in which we allow our minds to associate freely and the solution to emerge spontaneously. (That's why so many fresh ideas come to people in the shower or out for a walk or a run.)

The dubious gift of systems awareness

If people are given a quick view of a photo of lots of dots and asked to guess how many there are, the strong systems thinkers in the group tend to make the best estimates. This skill shows up in those who are good at designing software, assembly lines, matrix organizations, or interventions to save failing ecosystems—it's a very powerful gift indeed. After all, we live within extremely complex systems. But, suggests the Cambridge University psychologist Simon Baron-Cohen (a cousin of Sacha's), in a small but significant number of people, a strong systems awareness is coupled with an empathy deficit—a blind spot for what other people are thinking and feeling and for reading social situations. For that reason, although people with a superior systems understanding are organizational assets, they are not necessarily effective leaders.

An executive at one bank explained to me that it has created a separate career ladder for systems analysts so that they can progress in status and salary on the basis of their systems smarts alone. That way, the bank can consult them as needed while recruiting leaders from a different pool—one containing people with emotional intelligence.

Putting It All Together

For those who don't want to end up similarly compartmentalized, the message is clear. A focused leader is not the person concentrating on the three most important priorities of the year, or the most brilliant systems thinker, or the one most in tune with the corporate culture. Focused leaders can command the full range of their own attention: They are in touch with their inner feelings, they can control their impulses, they are aware of how others see them, they understand what others need from them, they can weed out distractions and also allow their minds to roam widely, free of preconceptions.

This is challenging. But if great leadership were a paint-by-numbers exercise, great leaders would be more common. Practically every form of focus can be strengthened. What it takes is not talent so much as diligence—a willingness to exercise the attention circuits of the brain just as we exercise our analytic skills and other systems of the body.

The link between attention and excellence remains hidden most of the time. Yet attention is the basis of the most essential of leadership skills—emotional, organizational, and strategic intelligence. And never has it been under greater assault. The constant onslaught of incoming data leads to sloppy shortcuts—triaging our e-mail by reading only the subject lines, skipping many of our voice mails, skimming memos and reports. Not only do our habits of attention make us less effective, but the sheer volume of all those messages leaves us too little time to reflect on what they really mean. This was foreseen more than 40 years ago by the Nobel Prize–winning economist Herbert Simon. Information "consumes the attention of its recipients," he wrote in 1971. "Hence a wealth of information creates a poverty of attention."

My goal here is to place attention center stage so that you can direct it where you need it when you need it. Learn to master your attention, and you will be in command of where you, and your organization, focus.

Originally published in December 2013. Reprint R1312B

About the Contributors

DEBORAH ANCONA is the Seley Distinguished Professor of Management at the MIT Sloan School of Management and the founder of the MIT Leadership Center.

ELAINE BACKMAN is a research affiliate at the MIT Leadership Center.

TIZIANA CASCIARO is a professor of organizational behavior at the University of Toronto's Rotman School of Management.

AMY C. EDMONDSON is the Novartis Professor of Leadership and Management at Harvard Business School and author of *The Fearless Organization* (Wiley, 2019).

SYDNEY FINKELSTEIN is the Steven Roth Professor of Management and the faculty director of the Center for Leadership at the Tuck School of Business at Dartmouth College. His latest book is *Superbosses: How Exceptional Leaders Master the Flow of Talent.*

DANIEL GOLEMAN, a codirector of the Consortium for Research on Emotional Intelligence in Organizations at Rutgers University, is the author of *Focus: The Hidden Driver of Excellence* (HarperCollins, 2013).

BORIS GROYSBERG is a professor of business administration at Harvard Business School. He is the coauthor (with Michael Slind) of *Talk, Inc: How Trusted Leaders Use Conversations to Power Their Organizations* (Harvard Business Review Press, 2012).

MORTEN T. HANSEN (mortenhansen@berkeley.edu) is a management professor at the University of California, Berkeley, School of Information, and at INSEAD. He is the author of *Collaboration: How Leaders Avoid the Traps, Create Unity, and Reap Big Results* (Harvard Business Review Press, 2009).

SAMANTHA HOWLAND, a senior managing partner at Decision Strategies International, leads its Executive and Leadership Development Practice.

HERMINIA IBARRA is the Cora Chaired Professor of Leadership and Learning and a professor of organizational behavior at INSEAD. She is the author of *Act Like a Leader, Think Like a Leader* (Harvard Business Review Press, 2015).

KATE ISAACS is a research affiliate at the MIT Leadership Center and a partner at Dialogos Generative Capital.

SUJIN JANG is an assistant professor of organizational behavior at INSEAD.

STEVE KRUPP is the CEO of Decision Strategies International.

MARIANNE W. LEWIS is the dean of Cass Business School at City University London.

NITIN NOHRIA is the dean of Harvard Business School.

MICHAEL E. PORTER is a University Professor at Harvard, based at Harvard Business School.

PAUL J.H. SCHOEMAKER is the founder and executive chairman of Decision Strategies International (DSI) and the research director of the Mack Center for Technological Innovation at the Wharton School.

MICHAEL SLIND is a writer, editor, and communication consultant. He is the coauthor (with Boris Groysberg) of *Talk, Inc: How Trusted Leaders Use Conversations to Power Their Organizations* (Harvard Business Review Press, 2012).

WENDY K. SMITH is an associate professor at the University of Delaware's Alfred Lerner College of Business & Economics.

MICHAEL L. TUSHMAN is the Paul R. Lawrence MBA Class of 1942 Professor of Business Administration at Harvard Business School. He and Wendy K. Smith have made paid presentations to W.L. Gore & Associates.

MICHAEL D. WATKINS is the chairman of Genesis Advisers, a professor at IMD, and the author of *The First 90 Days, Updated and Expanded* (Harvard Business Review Press, 2013).

Index

action, willingness to take, 135. *See also* nimble leadership

adhesives, 88. *See also* collaboration, horizontal

agenda
of CEOs, 105–108
pursuing an, 12–14

Akamai Technologies, 74–75

alignment, 37–38. *See also* strategic leadership

amygdala, 150, 157. *See also* self-awareness

Ancona, Deborah, 133–147

anticipate, ability to, 32–33

architecting leaders, 134, 141–144, 146

Athenahealth, 4–5

attention
direct, 149
power and, 159–160
strengthening, 152
toward others, 154–160
toward self, 149–154
to wider world, 160–162
See also focus

authenticity, 43–55

authentic selves, 150–151

autonomy, 138, 144–145

awareness
expanding your, 153
open, 151, 153, 161
self-awareness, 28, 149–152
systems, 162

Backman, Elaine, 133–147

Ballmer, Steve, 143

Baron-Cohen, Simon, 162

Becht, Bart, 77, 81

Beers, Charlotte, 54

Benioff, Marc, 71–72

boards of directors, 119. *See also* chief executive officers (CEOs)

Bock, Laszlo, 90

Bohr, Niels, 70

both/and leadership, 57–70

boundaries, 59–60

boundary crossing, 86–97

Boyatzis, Richard, 153

bridges, 87–88. *See also* collaboration, horizontal

Brinker, Norman, 126–127, 129, 131

business environment, 57–58, 65

buy-in, obtaining, 47–48

Campbell, Jeff, 126–127, 129

Carlucci, Alessandro, 78–79

Casciaro, Tiziana, 85–97

challenge, ability to, 33–35

Chambers, John, 9

change
economic change, 7
embracing, 65–66
generational change, 7
global change, 7
managing, 24
organizational, 7, 24, 65–66
technological change, 7

Chatter, 71–72, 78

chief executive officers (CEOs)
accessibility of, 116
agendas of, 105–108
alone time for, 116–117
constraints on, 121
direct reports of, 109–110
executive assistants of, 106–107
external constituencies of, 117–119
face-to-face interactions by, 103–105
importance of, 124
influence of, 119–122, 124
integrating mechanisms used by, 111–113

Engage with HBR content the way you want, on any device.

With HBR's new subscription plans, you can access world-renowned **case studies** from Harvard Business School and receive **four free eBooks**. Download and customize prebuilt **slide decks and graphics** from our **Visual Library**. With HBR's archive, top 50 best-selling articles, and five new articles every day, HBR is more than just a magazine.

Subscribe Today
hbr.org/success

The most important management ideas all in one place.

We hope you enjoyed this book from *Harvard Business Review*. Now you can get even more with HBR's 10 Must Reads Boxed Set. From books on leadership and strategy to managing yourself and others, this 6-book collection delivers articles on the most essential business topics to help you succeed.

HBR's 10 Must Reads Series

The definitive collection of ideas and best practices on our most sought-after topics from the best minds in business.

- Change Management
- Collaboration
- Communication
- Emotional Intelligence
- Innovation
- Leadership
- Making Smart Decisions

- Managing Across Cultures
- Managing People
- Managing Yourself
- Strategic Marketing
- Strategy
- Teams
- The Essentials

hbr.org/mustreads